REVELATION:

A Story for God's Children

Charles Boggs

Order From:

Charles Boggs
5065 Highway 19
Nichols, SC 29581

ISBN: 0-9640453-0-3

Produced by
JM Productions
Brentwood, TN 37024-1911

PRINTED IN THE UNITED STATES OF AMERICA

Contents

Introduction

There is greater reason today to believe in the imminent return of Christ than ever before. Simple logic would tell us we are closer to that return now than even yesterday. Yet, beyond logic, events seem to be rapidly unfolding for His Second Coming. Because of that, there is also greater interest to understand this Book entitled "Revelation."

Many have written on it before. Hal Lindsey, Billy Graham, David Jeremiah, and J. Vernon McGee are only a few of renowned men of God who have done extensive works about this Book. I refer you to them for their expertise. I invite you, though, to open your Bible and follow along for this stroll and view anew the pathways of God.

As we look at the world today, it is easy to become pessimistic. With all the problems from politics to world economics, from social to spiritual, from individual to global, it appears that Satan might be winning. What hope do we have?

The Bible is filled with hope. The very story of Christ's life brings hope. That He lived and resisted all temptation, that He defeated the power of sin and the results of death, that He lives now interceding for those who love Him—all these truths keep hope alive. But even with this hope of the past and present, what hope do we have that tomorrow Christ will continue to be our victorious hope?

The victory Christ won for us on the cross is a victory forever. The American Civil War was probably decided on the fields of Gettysburg, yet the war continued for many months afterward. The victory of the cross assures us of the victory of tomorrow, but does not relieve us of its battles. Those battles will not end until Christ comes again and establishes His kingdom once and for all.

There are many Scriptural references to this series of events. The prophetic Books of Daniel, Isaiah, and Malachi, along with even the Book of Psalms in the Old Testament, talk about both the first and second comings of Christ. Matthew, Mark, John, Acts, 1 Corinthians, and 2 Thessalonians give us additional prophecy of the culmination of Christ's triumph. Each of these has individual references that assure us of that ultimate victory, but no detail is given as to how, who, what, when, and where.

Only in one Book are we given a detailed view of the victory consummated. Because we have that one Book, we who truly believe in Jesus Christ as Savior and Lord, even though Satan appears to have control today, know that some day pay day will come.

When I was a senior in high school, our school had one of the best football teams in the state. But one night instead of being the strong, almost invincible, conquerors of the gridiron, our team found itself thwarted by a second-rate school. At halftime we were behind 21-0. The coach reminded the team that night that it was indeed only halftime. There were still plays to be made. Our team came back to win that game. We went into that game victors and came out victors. In between it was not easy. The Book of Revelation is much the same. For Christians today, we know the past victories, we have hope in the future one, but in between it will not be easy.

Before we look at the Book of Revelation we need to understand exactly what God is trying to tell each person who reads it. For the believer there should be no fear in reading this Book. Those who read it properly (with the guidance of the Holy Spirit) should instead be brought to a new experience of worship and wonder at God's love and to a new commitment to tell those who do not believe about Him.

For those who do not truly believe or have deceived themselves into thinking they have salvation, looking at this Book should elicit fear, trembling, and a desire for salvation. In the past many preachers have used this Book aimed at that one result: trying to scare the literal and real hell out of people. It is a Book of warning: warning of judgment to those who have rebelled against God and refuse His salvation. It contains horrors on such an unprecedented scale that our minds have difficulty taking it all in. It can scare you. It scared me until I realized who God was addressing with this message. H. Stephen Shoemaker once stated that the Book of Revelation is a children's story, designed to strengthen, mature, and guide God's children. The Book was written, not to the unbeliever, but to the believer, and as we plunge into this study we need to keep that in mind. All that God tells John to write, He is addressing to the believer, the church, the family of God.

The only reason this should scare you is *if you are not sure of your salvation or if you know of a loved one who is not saved.* John wrote this Book, not to scare but to reassure the believers of his day and those Christians of every generation until Christ returns.

John wrote Revelation under the inspiration of the Holy Spirit, after being severely persecuted for his faith. He wrote after watching the church he loved being tried, tortured, and systematically eradicated under one of the most vicious of all Roman emperors, Domitian. The message to the church then and now is that nothing can separate the believer from the love of God (see Rom. 8:35-39). Christ is still in control, no matter how bad it looks. The victory He won on Calvary will be finalized one day.

The title is "The Revelation of Jesus Christ," and that presents the theme. It is not a Book of "revelations" (as many often call it) but one of revealing—the revealing of Christ past, present, and future. There is a caution, a warning for those who study it and teach it given at the end of the writing (Revelation 22:18-19). Take time to mull over that warning and pray constantly for the guidance of the Holy Spirit as you study the rest of the Book. There is also a blessing given in it for those who read and study it (1:3). God never leaves us with a warning without also sharing His blessing for those who sincerely endeavor to follow Him.

To fully understand the Book of Revelation, you either need a good knowledge of the rest of Scripture or explanation as we go along. The reason there are so many crazy interpretations of this Book is that the interpreter does not consider the rest of Scripture. *The Bible* is the best commentary on the Bible. Scripture always agrees with itself. For this reason, there will be various Scriptural references listed and at times explained. Spend time reading them.

The purpose of this writing is not to join in the various arguments about pre- or post-tribulation theories or pre-, post-, or amillennial theories, but to clarify Scripture. To do this the viewpoint expressed will be a pre-tribulation viewpoint. Even if you consider this viewpoint wrong, in most cases the interpretation of the Scripture will still have validity.

Most people believe the Book of Revelation is simply the future events of history in relation to God. The book very neatly covers all history. Chapter 1 treats from before the beginning of time until the ascension of Christ. Chapters 2 and 3 cover the time of the church until the rapture, and the remaining chapters deal with time from the rapture until time is no more.

It is not a difficult Book for people today since unfolding history has clarified many of the visions. It covers all the major prophetic themes of the Bible, from Christ to Satan. It is probably the best-organized book of the Bible, being deliberately set out to walk us through time.

The difficulties that many claim to have with the Book generally revolve around the symbols that are mixed in with reality to create a masterpiece of prophecy. An example of that is clearly seen in the second and third chapters which cover church history. The reality is that John was writing to seven real and existing churches going through various trials and difficulties. Symbolically, each church represents an age in church history from the apostolic church to the apostate church.

A brief outline of the book would show the following:

Chapter 1: Christ Pre-existent to Glorified Ascension

Chapters 2 and 3: The Earthly Church History

Chapters 4 and 5: The Raptured Church in Heaven

Chapters 6 through 18: The Tribulation

Chapter 19: The Return of Christ

Chapter 20: The Millennial Reign

Chapters 21 and 22: Great White Throne and the Beginning of Eternity Future.

All of this centers on Jesus Christ. It is His revelation to His followers. It is an important book for the church today to know and understand for it declares that Christ is preparing to return. If He did return now, would He find us ready, working to make sure everyone we know had a chance to come in faith to Him? Believers today can draw hope from the knowledge that God is in control. What will happen will be horrible, but God still loves, still grants mercy to those who seek Him, and still securely provides for His own. The Book of Revelation will help to relieve worry, increase witnessing, challenge commitment, and increase church growth.

It is not a fairy tale or fictional horror story. What it says will literally happen. As Shoemaker expressed it in his book *Retelling the Biblical Story*, "At its most profound level this is a child's story. . . ." With that in mind let us pray for the guidance of the Holy Spirit through this factual story written by God for His children.

Chapter 1

Revelation 1: 1-20

The island of Patmos was Domitian's combination of Devil's Island, Alcatraz, and Auschwitz. On that small, barren piece of rock John, apostle and the most intimate of friends with Jesus of Nazareth, found himself imprisoned. His crime was simply believing and preaching that Jesus was the Christ, the Son of God sent to redeem all mankind. Domitian believed himself to be God and was intent on showing John and all like him his power. John had been tortured in many ways and finally placed in solitary confinement on Patmos.

Being the loving and concerned pastor John was, his thoughts there were not self-centered. He had moments when he wondered and even doubted about his life and faith, but his main concern was the others he had left behind, specifically the churches he had pastored around Ephesus. The people of those churches were under the severest of persecution. Thousands had already died. Thousands more had been tortured, seen family members carried off into slavery, watched their businesses and homes burned or confiscated by the government and given to the government's paid snitches. The agony of his love for the church was profound, and in the midst of that agony a messenger from God came.

On a Sunday, "the Lord's Day," in the midst of his prayer time, "The Revelation" started. It was a revelation of his Savior, directed to John through the Savior, then through an angel. John was to send it on to all the Church through the seven churches with whom he had close contact around Ephesus. It was to be a message of encouragement that would bless all who read it and believed. This blessing and encouragement was not simply the promise of John, but the gift of the complete Spirit of God (represented by the "seven spirits") endorsed by the everlasting Christ. It was to be about the eternal Christ who has always testified of the accurate and truthful precepts of God and who, because of His love shown by the giving of His life's blood on the cross, not only has provided forgiveness for sin, but is the rightful ruler of all, even the kings of this earth, even the wicked character named Domitian.

The good news given to John is that because of Christ those who believe in Him as Savior and Lord are now also elevated to rulers – kings and priests, leaders both physically and spiritually. And there will be no end to the reign we have because Christ lives eternally. Some may doubt this fact, but their doubt will end in fear when one day He returns, "and every eye will see Him."

John was aware of all this but on that special Lord's Day, he was reminded of it all by the exalted Christ Himself, "I have always been and always will be. What you see is real. It is what is happening now and what must happen in the future. It will happen suddenly, when people are the least prepared. It will happen exactly as I give it to you; nothing will change, for this is the will of the Father. Write it down, drawing pictures with symbolic and descriptive words, and send it to the seven churches you have been praying for, and then to all believers of all ages until I come to carry them with Me to heaven." He recognized it was Christ speaking, for it was a voice of authority sounding forth a trumpet call of assembly and alert to the Church of God. He knew the Spirit of God was working miraculously to allow him to see and hear this special message from God.

The voice ended long enough for John to turn and behold in front of him the Church represented by seven lampstands. In the center of them was Christ wearing a robe of royalty and the medals of victory on His chest. This was a vision of the complete Church (the number seven symbolic of completeness or wholeness). The Church's function from the time of John through history to the time of its rapture was to shine the light of truth to the world. This light came only from making Christ the center of their being and empowering the Church with His oil, the Holy Spirit. The light of truth was to go in every direction with clarity. To those whose light was clouded in smoke—the smoke of disobedience, laziness, and sin—Christ's standing in the midst was a warning that He knew everything the church was doing and why. He would be ready to cut through the smoke by trimming their wick, by disciplining them. If that did not work He stood ready to snuff out the individual lamps (churches) which continued in disobedience.

The appearance of Christ was one of purity of life and judgment. The whiteness of his hair showed him without sin, the fire in his eyes revealed He knew all—all the thoughts, motives, and inner secrets of each man, woman, and child. His feet like brass represented the strength of His coming judgment, a strength given to Him because He alone is without sin. That strength was reinforced by the voice of might and authority like the roar of a waterfall.

His lordship was shown by His holding in His right hand the symbolic stars of His true ministers, guiding and protecting them. His weapons of lordship were the very words spoken from His mouth, the Word of God given in Scripture to us. That Word is able to attack in one direction those who would deny Him and defend in the other direction those who would follow Him. John was overwhelmed by His radiance, as if he were looking directly into the sun. John collapsed to his knees in fear-filled speechless worship and adoration.

In a move of deepest compassion and love, Christ reached out to John, placing the same hand of guidance and protection for all His ministers on John and urging him once again not to be afraid. "This that you see, John, is Me. The One who lives forever. Since before time began I have been. You know Me because, in the perfect point of that time, I took human form, lived among men, and was rejected by them. You know Me as the One who lived and was killed, but you saw Me returned to life, and I will live forevermore. That has been affirmed by the Father. Because of my life, death, and resurrection, I have the authority over those who will live with Me and those who reject Me. I am about to reveal to you that authority. Write it all down, for My ministers to relate to the churches you love and through them to all churches I love. Let My message be clear and plain so all might have the opportunity to know and proclaim salvation."

References:

Philippians 2:9-11; 1 Peter 2:9; Hebrews 13:8; John 1:4-9; John 12:35-36; Isaiah 11:5; John 16:13-14; John 15:1-2; 1 Corinthians 11:27-32; Daniel 7:9; Hebrews 4:12-13; Daniel 10:6; John 5:28-29; Matthew 17:2; John 10:29-30; John 10:10

Chapter 2

Revelation 2: 1-29

With pen and parchment ready, John started to transcribe the letters from Christ to the seven churches. He was profoundly aware that these letters were more than personal words to these seven individual churches. He recognized that they would be Christ's evaluation of all churches and the signs of the seven Church ages to come.

"To the pastor of the church at Ephesus . . ." Vivid images of that church flowed through John's mind. Chief city of the province of Galatia, it was the center of both religious and commercial activity. It was a modern city with a social life that boasted an indoor theater that could seat 20,000 and an amphitheater that could seat over 100,000.

Life in Ephesus centered around the Temple of Diana, goddess of fertility. It was the largest Greek temple ever built with dozens of massive columns over five stories high. It was not simply a religious or worship center. It was a mall containing a bank, art gallery, shops, and even a court for handling various legal matters. But worship there was important and highly involved.

Worship centered on drunkenness, orgies, drugs, feasts, and the mystery religions that later generations would know as the occult. The temple was simply a miniature of the entire city of Ephesus, drawn to worldliness and sin.

The church had been established there by the powerful preacher Apollos. Paul of Tarsus encountered this church shortly after it began and helped the membership clear up some doctrinal problems. Under Paul's two-year ministry, God performed miracles to counter the influence of the mystery religions, but those miracles forced Paul to leave. Since that time the church had had two more pastors—a young man named Timothy and then John himself. Under those ministers, the church at Ephesus had become a hub from which direction and leadership to other churches in the province radiated.

To this church Christ revealed himself as the One without whom the church would not be. This church of power and influence was reminded that its very life came from Christ who even then was watching the church and analyzing it without favoritism. Christ saw good going on in the church at Ephesus. The people were working hard. Physically and numerically it was a growing congregation. The members worked diligently, patiently going through the trials of growth and persecution. Even when the times became rough and their bodies were fatigued, their spirits remained high.

The Ephesian church was especially vigilant in testing their leadership to make sure those who taught and led were true believers and on the right pathway. That vigilance was good, but it was also a sign of what Christ saw wrong in this church. They had left their "first love."

Those dedicated, hard-working people had moved their enthusiasm, devotion, and spirit from being centered in Christ to being enmeshed in the activity. They knew doctrine, Scripture, and the Gospel story, but they were merely going through the motions. The special feelings of love toward Christ and one another had been replaced by a zeal to be strictly and legally right and proper. For many in that church the worship experience was no longer worship—but ritual and even a burden.

Christ instructed the church to remember who and what is at the center of their life. Love started the church. Love maintained the church of Ephesus and should do so in every church throughout history. The church of Ephesus represents the Church through the ages that has lost its loving feeling. If the church has lost that loving feeling that presents joy, peace, freedom, and a spirit of agape love, then it has left its first and only real love.

It was similar to a marriage relationship. Originally the couple had courted, and everything was special. Throughout the wedding ceremony and the honeymoon the love grew and flourished. Special things had been done from flowers and gifts to the holding of hands and sitting close together. The priority of the couple was their love for each other, and nothing would stand in the way of that love. They would rearrange their schedule to be with each other. No barrier was so great that it could keep them apart.

But love was replaced by routine, and routine, with ritual, and suddenly it is not a marriage based on love, but one based on habit, custom, and even legalism. The couple no longer had the special feelings, gifts, and acts. The priority was no longer on their love, but on jobs, children, housework, and entertainment. The marriage existed, but in name only because love was not at its center.

The church had become like that. Instead of holding hands and sitting close to Jesus, the members were content just to be somewhere nearby spiritually. Instead of rearranging schedules to be with others in worship, they let the world's schedule take over. The special feelings of church were gone. The church existed in name only.

Yet, there was hope for the church of Ephesus. Repentance from conceit, vanity, legalism, and ritualism were possible. Repentance from status consciousness to Christ consciousness was available and still is available. There is no such person as a "blue-blooded" Christian, one who is better than the rest. The only blood of the church is the blood of Christ which shows that all of us are sinners saved by grace.

If the church of Ephesus refused to repent, then it would be removed, its light snuffed out by Christ. If it would repent, it would be rewarded with a fresh filling of the Spirit of God that would provide strength to overcome all temptations. It would also possess wisdom about how to handle those who would lead the church body astray with false teachings and doctrine. The ultimate reward would be a confirmation of the eternal life guaranteed to each believer, a surety made perfect when the believer meets the Savior face to face.

As John recorded those words, he wondered if this church he knew so well would heed the words of Christ or be snuffed out. History would show that this church would be a description of the phase of church history from the ascension of Christ and Pentecost until approximately 100 A.D. History would also reveal that the local church at Ephesus would die, a warning from Christ having gone unheeded.

"To the pastor of the church at Smyrna . . ." John knew this church almost as well as the one at Ephesus. Smyrna was a seaport north of Ephesus that had one of the largest Jewish populations of all the cities in the area. It had a beautiful harbor and a multitude of temples to gods such as Zeus, Aphrodite, Apollo, and even one to the current Caesar. In that temple to Caesar, with a seating capacity of over 20,000 people, modern music was first performed. Some of the harshest persecution of the church's members was perpetrated there.

Smyrna was a proud city with a population that was status conscious. The local citizens were so intent on being socially acceptable, it did not matter who or what was sacrificed to climb the social ladder. The city had received its name from its large local crop of myrrh, a bitter plant used to make pain killers and embalming fluid. Myrrh actually meant "bitter," and it would be symbolic of the plight of the local church that would be one of the most persecuted in history.

Yet with all the persecution the church endured, the church of Smyrna was a picture of what Christ desired in His bride, an active, dynamic witness to Him in all situations. The members of this church loved Christ enough to stand openly and witness actively for their Savior, even if it meant sacrifice on their part. As John wrote the letter of Christ to this church, he quickly realized that for this faithful church enduring the trials and pains of oppression, there would be no rebuke or condemnation.

Christ reassured this church by identifying Himself as the eternal, living Lord who, having always existed and, even though killed by man, lives again and would forever. To the status-conscious people of Smyrna this revelation would affirm that only Christ was number one. No one could reach higher than His position. It would also reassure His followers that He is in control. No matter what might happen, even physical pain and death, He has defeated them all. He lives forever, and those who follow him would also live forever. For those who did not follow Him, who were involved in any way in the persecution of His followers from active participation to simple complacency, there would be judgment by the One in control who remains number one.

This church was under extreme pressure. Knowing this, Christ gave them additional words of commendation. The members were refusing to worship Caesar. They could have avoided all persecution merely by publicly swearing allegiance to the Caesar. All it required was a short phrase: "Caesar is Lord." But they refused and in the process lost their homes, jobs, families and lives.

They now lived in poverty with little or no hope of being able to work. Parents watched as children were carried off into slavery, as wives were attacked and mutilated. Children sat helpless as their parents and grandparents were roasted, boiled in oil, or crucified. But through it all they kept on assembling to worship, pray, sing praises, and witness boldly for their Lord.

Added to their persecution by the Roman government was the gleeful participation of the Jewish population in making sure that the Christians were wiped out. Those Jews claimed a relationship with God that was at best a convenient label. They found that turning against the Christians took the heat of persecution off them, plus there was an additional bonus. Anyone turning in a Christian to the authorities would receive a minimum of 10 percent of their property and wealth. Many Jews joined the church just to be spies so they could "rat" on true believers.

Christ urged this church to have no fear. All of this persecution was being instigated by Satan, and he had already been defeated on the cross. The persecution they were enduring would be short-term compared to eternity. History records that this particular persecution of all churches and believers lasted about 200 years. It was a time of terror and also of valor. To the victor Christ promises a crown showing the victory and the sacrifice made by these martyrs.

To the victor, the true believer, was a further promise that the suffering experience would never be experienced by them again. To the persecutors, the suffering they inflicted would be inflicted upon them throughout eternity. The atrocity of death they had inflicted on the church would be only slight indication of the second death they would experience for eternity.

The church of Smyrna became a testimony of true faith to believers for all time. John had known personally many of those who would die for their faith. One was a student of his, a man named Polycarp. Polycarp would become pastor of this church, and at the age of 86 would be dragged into the temple of Caesar and commanded to deny his faith and give allegiance to Caesar. His refusal recorded in church tradition would express Christ's words well. While they prepared to burn him alive, his tormentors piling wood around him, Polycarp addressed them: "You threaten me with fire that burns for an hour, and this is gone. But you have willfully and purposefully denied the fire of the coming judgment . . . the fire of eternal punishment reserved for those who deny the only true God."

Smyrna's letter from Christ gave to us a prophecy of church history from 100 A.D. to 312 A.D. when the official persecution of Christianity by Rome came to an end.

"To the pastor of the church at Pergamos . . ." Pergamos was the official capital of the area known today as Asia Minor. At the time of John's vision from heaven it was dominated by several temples built into the side of the mountain that had been developed into the city. One of these temples was in fact a library that boasted at one time an inventory of over 200,000 writings which Mark Antony had presented to Cleopatra as a gift. These

writings had been the origin of the city's name, Pergamos, the proper name of parchment.

The greatest minds of John's day had connections with this city. Those minds had developed various ideas about religion, including a religion involved with healing and medicine. With so many religions around, there was always a debate as to which one was the best or even real.

To this church Christ revealed Himself as the two-edged sword, an instrument that would open up any adversaries to the truth. Christ was reaffirming His followers that He and He alone is the only true God. His Word reveals Him as such and silences any opposition.

The church at Pergamos had undergone its share of trouble. With all the other religious beliefs, cultic in nature, and with Caesar still wanting people to give their allegiance solely to him, this church had maintained its faith and works amid a very hostile environment. There were people with more education, power, influence, and wealth, always trying to silence that group of Christians. But those Christians would not be silenced, and even dared to vocalize their faith even more.

Circumstances were so bad in Pergamos that Christ equated the city with Satan's throne. Religious activity outside of God and Christ is a ruse of the devil, a center of his lies. The Temple of Bacchus, the god of wine, actually gave us an image of Satan. The god was a combination of man and beast, having the head and upper torso of a man, with horns and cloven feet from some animal. It is interesting that the god of wine (alcohol) is shown as one of our images of Satan.

Another religion of tremendous power and influence centered at the Temple of Aesculapius. This temple was actually a type of hospital, allowing for certain physical cures, along with psychological treatment that compares easily with modern self-help philosophy. Treatment included massages, steam baths, and lectures on being all you can be and thinking yourself not only into better health, but into better positions in life. There was also the ultimate in scare-tactic type therapy. If all else failed you were treated by having to walk, or even crawl, through a dimly lit room full of snakes. Our modern symbol used by physicians contains the idol-symbol of this temple, snakes twisted around a pole.

All of these cultic religious beliefs took on the titles of "mystery religions," because so much was considered a secret in how matters were performed. Confronting them was the "mystery" of God revealed in Christ that threatened them all. The martyrs from the church at Pergamos were many. One of the first to be martyred, Antipas, Christ mentioned by name to John, an indication of Christ's personal involvement with every breath of an individual's life.

Although the church had maintained a witness for Christ, John was instructed by Him to inform this church that it had failed in one major area. They had been seduced by the pagan religions. Christ compared this seduction to the seduction of Israel by Balaam. The church was allowing other faiths and beliefs to infiltrate and pollute their worship. They were adopting procedures and ceremonies from them and even baptizing people who were not truly saved. In addition they continued to allow leaders of the mystery religions to teach their beliefs in the church. This was not a quest for knowledge so they could convert the unsaved. This was a compromise with them.

Many beliefs were now accepted from these cults and pagan religions. Among them was the belief that the only way to secure one's salvation was by continuing to live in sin—the bigger the sinner you were, the greater your salvation, a theory voiced by a group called the Nicolaitans. This was the idea that only a priest had access to Christ and that God elevated the clergy and silenced the doctrine of the priesthood of the believer. The church had compromised itself with the world, an act Christ equated with adultery. Christ's warning to this church was clear. Repent or He would declare war with His two-edged sword. His Word would expose the truth, what is correct and not, what is real faith and what is the deception of Satan.

For those who repented, who did truly trust in Christ, there would be a revelation of the mystery of God which would make the mystery religions pale into insignificance. There would be a spiritual feeding of heavenly rations (manna) that would aid in the growth spiritually and physically of the church. And to counter the mystery religions' tendency to send secret and hidden messages, Christ would provide each believer with a spiritual identification, a white stone showing they were His. This stone John would recognize as the stone of innocence, given to someone on trial. The Roman courts gave black stones to the guilty and white to those found innocent. Christ symbolized His followers' innocence because of faith. By faith you have been pardoned, given a new life with a new Lord, and a new relationship with Him shown by a new name.

John could see the compromise coming in his day. I am sure his prayer, as he transcribed the message of the Lord, was that the church would also see it and repent. History relates that a few did, but that churches (not just the local one at Pergamos) all compromised with the Roman government starting in the year 312 A.D. Under the deceptive practices of Constantine, Christianity was made the official religion of Rome and required for all citizens, whether they believed or not. Clergy were elevated to political power, and the rule of Constantine was combined to control the church under the guise of a new title, "Vicar of Christ and Pope." In Greek the term "vicar" has at times been translated as "anti."

Under the new Roman combined church, later called Roman Catholic, temples formerly used to worship idols were changed to churches, and the idols were given new names of saints that were supposed to have influence over Christ, even to the performing of miracles. This phase of Church history would continue until approximately 590 A.D.

The persecution of the Church was over for a time. The Roman government had finally achieved what it had tried to do for over 200 years—defeat the Christians by compromise. Spiritual adultery was the crime, and Christ's Word continues to reveal it to us today for what it is. His Word also still provides us an opportunity to repent and believe the truth.

"To the pastor of the church at Thyatira . . . " In his time as pastor John had a deep concern for this church. It had never grown like the others around it and would be the smallest of all the churches that Christ directly addressed. The faith, commitment, and discipleship of this church never developed.

Thyatira was a military town, built as a defensive position to at least impede invading armies before they could reach the more important cities of Ephesus, Smyrna, and Pergamos. Over the years this town had become famous for its blue-collar workers who had organized themselves into guilds, unions, or lodges. Although the military presence was important, the town had developed commerce around wool and dyes. John had well known an owner of one of the dye companies, a woman named Lydia whom Paul had encountered in Philippi.

The trade unions, guilds, and lodges came to wield a power second only to the Roman government. To get a job, make money, buy, sell, trade, and even have a social life, you had to be a member of one of those guilds. They had started off with good intentions designed to promote the welfare of the membership and to be involved in community projects. They had evolved into power-hungry entities with religious undertones. At the time of John they even had religious-type services, performing funerals, weddings, and worship services based on certain gods involved in mystery religions. They had secret codes, signs, and symbols that only the membership knew and understood.

When Christianity came to the town, the guilds incorporated this new religion of Christianity into their practices and found it gained respectability among Christians. The church actually had its members joining with these pagan practices.

To this church Christ showed Himself to be the Son of God, the only One to whom allegiance is due—to Christ and Christ alone is the believer's loyalty and oath. Christ also revealed Himself as the One who sees beyond the outward facade of a person's life to the inner being and motive. With eyes of flame He penetrates into the core and soul of our being and there judges what He finds. For those who compromise, who have motives of service outside of love for Christ, who appear devoted but are really no more than playing a game with Christianity, there will come judgment.

This church was reminded, as all churches should be, that Christ is constantly watching, analyzing, and reacting to every thought, deed, and plan of the Church and its individual members.

Christ asked John to commend this church in several areas. Its works, charity, service, faith, and patience, even at times of difficulty, showed a certain depth of faith, love, and commitment. They were persistent. Even when tired and weary, they kept on going and giving. This had caused some growth, but it was superficial because the disease of compromise was still in the church, eating away at the areas of strength the church still possessed.

Christ compared this church's compromise with Jezebel. Apparently the church actually had a "Jezebel" in its midst, an unbeliever teaching believers and inducing them to go further down the road of concession. Her teaching centered in what some mystery religions claim even to this day to be "reality." "Reality" means that you cannot really have a separate belief. If you are, the world labels you as strange, weird, or snobbish. The world insists that you must be part of "the crowd" or, in the case of Thyatira, the guild to get along; to really win people you have to give in to certain things; and the final "reality" is it's OK to worship God, but one doesn't need Christ. Further, any belief in God will get you to heaven. He is all love and would never allow anyone who sincerely tried to worship Him go to a place like hell. That is the view of "New Age" religion to this day.

The pressure to conform was great from the lodges, the false leadership, and from society. This church gave in to the pressure. Christ warned them and the false leaders including "Jezebel" to repent while they had time. That warning was: everything about "Jezebel's" life would become sick, from physical illness to spiritual illness. Those who allowed her and those like her to continue to influence the church would also suffer. Whether they openly endorsed the false teaching or were simply too lazy or scared to stand against it, those who allowed compromise would also suffer. If coming close to God, if changing your life-style to fit God's plans is too much for you to do, God declared you will suffer because of your lack of faith, commitment, and love.

The believers in this false teaching, even though superficially members of the church, would suffer eternally. Those who stand against false teaching would not suffer an additional burden of suffering. The suffering they were enduring in their earthly life would not continue for eternity. Christ urged the true believer to "hang in there." One day He is coming back to carry His church home with Him. Those who truly follow Him will have no further tribulation. When they are carried to their eternal home they will rule with Christ. The guilds and world systems that are in control today will be replaced by the Lordship of Christ, and believers will rule with Him. They will be part of Him, stars in the heavenly family.

John could not have realized exactly how far the church would compromise. This letter addressed that phase of church history from 590 AD to 1517 A.D. During this time of the Dark Ages the Roman Catholic Church consolidated its power by further compromise with the world's ways. The doctrines – involving icons, the worship of the Virgin, mass for the dead, purgatory, and priestcraft, using ritual to replace spirit and faith – were instituted into the church to deceive many. The church in its supposed zeal to protect the faith became power-hungry and persecuted its own. Hundreds of thousands of true believers were martyred by the Roman Catholic Church in inquisitions that rival Hitler's "Final Solution" that we refer to today as "The Holocaust."

To this church God has shown patience. He has given it time and space in which to repent. What John wrote I am sure brought tears to his eyes then, as it should to ours now. There is still time to repent in truth, but those involved in this type of church who truly repent will be few in number.

References:

The Church at Ephesus . . .Titus 1:16; Ephesians 2:8-10; Matthew 5:16; 2 Corinthians 12:10; Revelation 22:2

The Church at Smyrna . . . Revelation 1:17-18, 20:14, 21:8; Matthew 10:17-18, 24:9; Luke 21:12; John 12:25, 15:20-21; Ephesians 2:4-7; James 1:12 ; 2 Timothy 2:12

The Church at Pergamos . . . Revelation 1:16; Hebrews 4:12-16; 1 Peter 5:8; Numbers Chapters 22 through 25; 2 Corinthians 6:14; Matthew 5:17; Romans 12:1-2; 2 Timothy 3:14-17; John 6:32-35,50-58; 1 Corinthians 13:12; Acts 17:23; Revelation 3:12

The Church at Thyatira . . . Acts 16:14; Revelation 1:14; James 2:18; 1 Corinthians 6:2; Revelation 22:16

Chapter 3

Revelation 3: 1-22

Four of the churches had been addressed. The messages to them candidly revealed how Christ peered beyond superficiality into the deepest heart of each part of His church. John surely recognized that all the churches throughout the ages would benefit from the messages he was being given. He prayed that they would indeed hear them and apply them to their lives.

"To the pastor of the church at Sardis . . ." In the mind of John there formed a picture of the church established in the city on top of a tall plateau. The city of Sardis was considered impregnable by the best of military minds, if only a small defense force was on duty there. The people of the city felt safe, secure, and happy in their walled city with only one steep, climbing road to enter its gates.

Sardis was the city of the mint. Gold had been discovered in the valley below many years before, and from that discovery had come the minting of coins for the government. Tremendous wealth resulted because of the combination of gold and security. Industry grew in the city to the extent that it actually started to outgrow its mountain top. All that Sardis did seemed to turn to gold. The legend of King Midas may have started in this boom town.

As impenetrable and safe as it was, Sardis had been conquered twice, and Christ's letter to the church used those two defeats as a foundation.

Christ identified Himself to this church as the One with the seven Spirits or the Holy Spirit. The Holy Spirit is the empowering agent of the Church. For the Church to genuinely be alive, dynamic, and functioning as Christ desires, it must be totally indwelt by the Spirit of God. Short bursts or revivals that end up in long periods of lethargy are not the indwelling of the Spirit—but only a sampling!

Christ told this church He was willing to provide spirit, energy, leadership, and all other resources necessary to do His will, but a church must desire the Spirit.

As John wrote these words of commendation to the church he realized that there was not much praise in them. Christ acknowledged the members had been doing some things a church should. Some sort of ministry was still occurring, at least in name, but that ministry was not being done in the power of the Spirit. Because of that the ministry was not being productive. Does that sound familar?

The church was having worship services as a formality. Worship and service had no real part of their assemblies. They were having activities with little or nothing to do with Christ. Meetings were held in which neither Christ nor God were mentioned, consulted in prayer, nor thought about. Many activities were more intent on food and fun than on what the church really was about. And through it all they called it worship. Habit and tradition were better terms for what evolved. Love, devotion, praise, and spiritual growth were hard to find. They had become the church of the "nominal" Christian.

John was all too familar with this type of church. He had walked into them and sensed that the Spirit was not there. The services were dull and dry. The people were satisfied so long as no one "rocked the boat" and stirred up any type of event that caused them to have to do anything extra. They had accomplished a little and thought it was a lot. They had their spiritual trophies, people won to the Lord, and were content to display them. There was no further need to win more, try harder, go farther.

When these words of complaint from Christ were directed to this church, John was not at all surprised. "You have a reputation of being something great, a vast growing hotbed of church activity. Your reports to the associational and convention offices look great. You always have a bunch of numbers, but you do not have a bunch of souls. Your reputation is a lie. You are not a living part of my body, but a dying, useless section. You can be revived if you repent quickly."

How can a dead church come back to life? Have you ever fallen asleep in a strange position and had an arm or leg go numb? The way to get "life" back into that limb is to restore the blood flow. A dead church is one that has restricted the blood flow. They have forgotten the blood that flowed on Calvary, the sacrifice of God's Son. They have forgotten the source of power and life, the Holy Spirit. They have forgotten what makes them a church—Christ being at the center of all they are in every aspect of their corporate and individual lives.

Sardis was dead because the members relied on a past reputation that was a present-day deception. Because they had not remained close to God through His Spirit, they had allowed sin to move into the membership to such a degree that Christ could state that only a few had not "soiled their garments" or given in to a sinful life. Finally they were dead because they had grown insensitive to their own spiritual condition. Now they refused to be honest with themselves about where they stood.

In record numbers churches today follow after Sardis. They become content, lethargic, satisfied, and complacent. They no longer confront sin in their midst but, fearful of offending some "brother" or "sister" in the membership, hide behind the Scripture of not judging one another. Then when some pastor or evangelist has the unmitigated gall to try to show them what is happening, they become angry, pout, claim the messenger from God is crazy, and ignore him. If you get mad at God's messenger (*if* he is God's messenger) then you are getting mad at God. Think about that.

God warned Sardis to wake up to the facts and to return to duty. The two times this "impregnable" city was conquered it was because the guards at the gate fell asleep. The enemy merely walked into the gates because the guards did not care enough to remain even half-alert. The church at Sardis suffered the same syndrome. They had become too lazy to do anything. They trusted that someone else, or even God, would do everything. They simply did not care, and many churches would follow their example.

Christ's stern warning was to wake up, strengthen what they had, and to reapply themselves to the task. They *knew* doctrine, Scripture, prayer, discipleship, and evangelism. They *knew* them, but did not *do* them. In the past they had. In the past they had stood tall for their Lord, sacrificing all if necessary. But the past was only that . . . *past*. But the job was still there to carry on.

To those who would repent and turn back to God there was Christ's promise of a robe of righteousness and a name that would live with them forever. There is a veiled warning in this letter, one that does not readily become clear until you look deep into the heart of God's love. The reference to the name in the book of life gives a clear warning that some who are members of the local church may not be members of the body of Christ.

Unless a person has been "born again," indwelt by the Holy Spirit, and confirmed in their salvation by that Spirit, it does not matter how many churches he joins, services he attends, positions he holds. He is just as lost as the person who never joined the church at all. Make sure of your salvation. Do not fall asleep or be content in some possible superfluous action of the past. Carefully, sincerely, and honestly ask yourself, "Am I absolutely sure that I am saved? Am I really and truly sure that if I died now I would go to heaven? What or who am I trusting for salvation?" If you have never given your heart and soul to Christ, do so now. Do not be deceived by the past. Claim the future. If you are not sure of your salvation, make sure of it (see 2 Pet. 1:10). Make sure by claiming again—maybe for the first time, in reality—salvation by grace through faith in Jesus Christ (see Eph. 2:8-9). Repent of your sins, trust in the Christ of now and forever, and follow Him.

The letter to the church at Sardis had a strange historical application. It is actually the letter of the Protestant Reformation which occurred from 1517 to 1750. It was a reformation that stopped short. Most Protestant denominations do not realize that they have stopped short of Christ's desire. Some short spurts of revival have taken place, but they have become bogged down in denominational wars, trying to organize better than the next denomination or to outdo one another with claims of being more evangelical, more "spiritual," more liberal, or conservative. It is sad that we have been lulled into a state of false contentment and even spiritual sleep because of what we claim (in many cases a claim without foundation) to have accomplished. When will God's people wake up to being more enthusiastic for Him?

"To the pastor of the church at Philadelphia . . ." It had been established as a border town to help spread Greek culture. Bordering three other districts, it had throughout its history suffered from various territorial disputes. It was also built on a natural fault line, subjecting it to some severe earthquakes.

One of those earthquakes had destroyed Philadelphia in 7 A. D. With no foreign-aid programs and no insurance system in operation, the city was left with little or no hope. But the Caesar of Rome stepped in, adopted the city, and sent vast amounts of personal aid to help rebuild it. Because of that it had taken a new name, *Neocaesareas*, the "new city of Caesar." It had a very active Jewish population, who claimed they were the only way to God. They held the "Keys of David," a Scriptural reference to having the authority of letting someone into the kingdom.

The main industry was the making of wine. The major problem of this city was inevitably, alcoholism. It also had an overabundance of pagan and mystery religions, claiming to be the only true religions and promising unbelievably immense rewards for those who followed them.

The church that John knew in Philadelphia identified well with the city. It was made up of people like the city itself, destroyed with no hope because of sin. The King of kings stepped in with grace and love and paid the total price for their restoration to life. Because of that, the members had a new name.

To this church John was commanded to identify Christ as the *only* authority, the *only* Lord, the *only* Way. He was not a fake. Those who followed Him, He would love, care for, and give deeply meaningful life. He identified Himself further as the real Key of David that has the power to open doors that no man can ever shut. This door is the door of salvation and opportunity for service that can only be opened by Christ. He also has the power to shut doors that no man can open. This is His power to judge. He judges in pure holiness and love. Those who fail to accept His provision of power cannot be saved by doing good works, having people pray for them after they die, or any of a myriad of other actions people claim can elevate them to heaven (see Titus 3:5).

Christ's words of praise for this church are marvelous. He declared He had opened many doors of opportunity for them, and they had not failed to go through them in faith. For that church in a border town, those opportunities to spread the Gospel must have been many. The members daily encountered people from all over the Roman empire with whom they could share the thrilling story of Christ.

The opportunities had been many; for this church, they had been a challenge on their physical resources. Although they had only a little, they took what they had and gave it their all to fulfill the prime directive of Christ to carry the words of salvation to the entire known world.

Their zeal had been met with anger; persecution had become terrible in almost overwhelming waves. Yet, with all the difficulties of lack of resources within and persecution from without, they had remained faithful. They still unashamedly and fearlessly proclaimed Jesus Christ as Savior, Lord, and Messiah.

Some of the most intense persecution came from what Christ identified as the "Synagogue of Satan," His name for the Jewish population in town that rejected Him. These Jews had done all they could to silence the believers. Christ would one day answer these actions against His own by vindicating the believers. Their faith will be shown as real when He returns. Those who persecuted would become persecuted, not only for a short time, but forever! Christ gave a glorious promise to this church that is a promise to His entire true Church. He prophesied that they would experience a mighty deliverance. They would not go through the tribulation. They would be kept from that hour of trial that would come suddenly.

When He comes again, He guaranteed, His followers will have a special place of worship and service in His new heaven and earth. They would not be subject to the ordeals and temptations of this sinful world anymore. They would be part of the family of God and carry the family name proudly. They would be citizens, not only of His kingdom, but of the capital city of His kingdom, the new Jerusalem. They would be close to Him in His rule and intimate with Him in joint ministry.

John wrote these words with a thrill in his heart and soul. No more trials, suffering, and pain. Each believer would remain a VIP in Christ's realm. And this church that was so intent on reaching others in His name received no words of warning or failure against it. For churches through the ages, the message was clear. If you constantly and lovingly proclaim the Lord, He will provide, guide, and love. For those who reach out to others in His name, heralding salvation available free of charge, Christ has nothing but words of praise. The assignment He has given us is not easy, but it is glorious (see Matt. 28:18-20).

The historical application of this church is the time from 1750 to the first half of the twentieth century. During this time the church became involved in worldwide missions and movements with such evangelists and preachers as John Wesley, William Carey, Billy Sunday, George Truett, and D. L. Moody. The Church had finally taken a step away from the traditions of the Reformation, but it was a step that was short-lived.

"To the pastor of the church at Laodicea . . ." As John prepared to take down the words of this message to the seventh church, he was reminded that the address of each message indi-

cated that the pastor was responsible for the well-being of the church. John hoped that the pastors he had helped become established understood that one day they would answer for their ministry. If they served with an open, loving, committed heart, Christ would reward them for it with a special crown. If done for an ego trip, power, personal glory, or advancement, they would be accountable to the Final Auditor one day.

Of all the cities around, Laodicea was the most prosperous. It was proud of its three major roles as a financial center, clothing manufacturing center, and a medical center with a university that had become famous for its healing eye salve. Situated on three major Roman roads, this city, in the center of the province of Galatia, was a busy hub for travelers heading by land from the east to Greece and Rome.

One of its biggest endeavors as a city was to establish a water system based on two major aqueducts. The original idea was for one aqueduct to go up into the mountains above the city and tap into the cold mountain waters, thus piping them into the city. The other aqueduct was going to the hot springs several miles across the nearby hills to carry hot water into the city. If these systems worked it would be the first major city-wide hot and cold water in the world. Unfortunately, the system, though costing a fortune, ended up a failure. The aqueducts had to be so long that, by the time the cold water reached the city it was lukewarm, and the hot water had cooled to the same undesirable state.

In this city of commerce, science, and advanced thinking the church had originally shown exceptional promise. But the letter Christ dictated to John showed that something had happened since the church was founded. Christ identified Himself as the "Amen," a term used as a proper noun only this one time in Scripture. He was emphasizing "I am the real affirmation of truth, the last word that can be trusted." As the Amen, then He could be trusted both to provide for those who followed Him and to judge fairly those who did not.

He also stated He was the "faithful and true Witness," analyzing the hearts and souls of those in the church and speaking to them the truth in love. He further pointed out He was the beginning of all creation, meaning He alone is the source of life, wealth, happiness, joy, peace, and love. From beginning to end He is God. He is God, and He alone encompasses life. He alone knows all, not just the facts, but also the reasons behind the facts. He is God.

As Christ looked upon the church at Laodicea He could find nothing that was right. He could not even begin to praise them as He had Sardis, which at least was going through some of the right motions. Christ called the church "lukewarm," and for John and the members of that church the failed aqueduct system came to mind. So many hopes, so much time, effort, and money had been invested into that which was supposed to provide refreshment, soothing, cleansing power, and new meaning and joy. But what was supposed to be hot and cold came out the same as the rest of the world's water supply, except worse. What they had was an expensive common water supply.

The church was the same. So much had been invested for it, to the point of the sacrifice of God's Son – so many hopes for new life, refreshment, joy, and meaning. But by the time the members of the church got around to doing what they should be doing for Christ, they were like the rest of the world. They had become indifferent, not only toward themselves, but toward others. These who supposedly claimed as Lord the Beginning of creation and the Last Word of life were mumbling, "So what?"

Christ taught it was better to be cold than lukewarm. That must have shocked John at first. It is better to be dead than just a warm body! Why? A cold person can be revived. A cold person may realize they are cold and will seek out warmth. Perhaps there is nothing worse than freezing to death, except spending eternity roasting in the fires of hell. Cold people will at least listen to ideas about warming up.

Lukewarm people are happy where they are. They do not want to be on fire. That requires giving up too much of the world to which they have grown accustomed. They do not want to be cold, because they have a certain amount of pride in what they have done—not what God has done but what they have done. They claim the church as their own. How many times John heard people do that and the echoes of their voices have haunted many a church since then! "This is my church, and we won't have young people messing it up." "This is my church, and we won't have those types of people joining." "This is my church, and as long as I'm alive we will never do it that way."

When will people learn, they do not own the church. If you are a Christian, Christ owns you. He bought and paid for you, a price that was too high for you to pay. When you become part of His Church, you follow Him and owe your all to Him, including control and dominion of your life.

John shivered as Christ gave warning to this church and all who followed in its footsteps. This church made Christ literally want to throw up. Spiritually afflicted churches make Christ ill.

In this town famous for money, clothes, and eye salve, the church was reminded of true wealth, raiment, and sight according to the One who knows *and is* the truth. They thought they had money, but they were really bankrupt. They thought they had put on the garments of the wedding feast, the robes of righteousness, but they were spiritually nude. They thought they could see the truth, especially since they had been healed by a salvation experience. But the salve they used was materialism and worldliness, and that ointment only blinds. All that the city of Laodicea was famous for was symbolically used to show that the only truth, the only fame, the only glory, and wealth are Christ's.

Christ called for them to repent. True wealth does not come from the bank but from the throne of grace. True raiment does not emerge from the department store but from the washing done in the blood of Christ. True vision does not proceed from eye drops but from blood drops that remove spiritual blindness.

For those who truly repented, Christ would provide what they would have to give up. You do not lose giving up the world's ways. You win because the victory is already secure. Repentance, true repentance, would be shown in a zeal that would boil over in the individual's life and, in the process, touch the Church. Christ made it plain that we can tell if someone is truly saved, if they honestly repent, dedicate themselves, and follow Him. They will be as obvious as an old tea kettle boiling on the stove, singing the songs of the redeemed at the top of their lungs, ready to be poured out to offer blessing to others.

Christ closed this letter with a statement of His patience. Down through history many have accepted what John wrote to close this letter and applied it as an invitation for the unsaved to receive Christ. He is standing at the doorway of their heart, asking, knocking, pleading to be let in as Lord, Savior, Friend, and Elder Brother. This application is true, but the letter John took down was written to the Church, to believers, not unbelievers. The Church and the individuals that make it up must recognize that right now Christ is knocking on the doorway to the deeper parts of your life. Right now He desires to be let into a closer relationship, one that boils over instead of just lowly simmers. He wants a relationship that is "on fire," not one that is barely smoking. He wants a relationship that really lives, not one that constantly requires shock treatments to make that spiritual heart beat again. Right now He is asking those who believe to repent of the sin, the complacency, the lethargy, the self-centeredness that is making them nauseating to Christ.

Historically speaking, the church at Laodicea represents the Church of today that will be in existence until the rapture. Today's Church, with a few exceptions, is lukewarm about Spirit-motivated missions, evangelism, and discipleship. Somewhere along the road of salvation the Church has been led down the path of world affairs. The Church today can enlist hundreds to go out and lie in front of an abortion clinic, but it can induce only a handful to go out witnessing positively for Christ. Maybe if we started doing the things of Christ again, we would not have to block clinics, demonstrate in front of government buildings, and campaign so hard against violence and sex in television and music. Maybe if we followed the Great Commission of Matthew 28:19-20 we could cut down on shelters for the homeless because the homeless would be won to the Lord and desire to become part of working society again. Maybe if we became fired up for Christ, we would again find the truth that would really set us free (see John 8:32).

References:

The Church at Sardis . . . Revelation 1:4; Luke 10:20; Philippians 4:5; Daniel 12:1; Luke 12:8-9

The Church at Philadelphia . . . John 1:9; John 14:6; John 15:1; Isaiah 22:20-25; John 5:29; Ephesians 2:8-10; James 2:8; 2 Corinthians 12:9; Luke 19:10; John 20:21; John 14:23; Acts 17:11; 2 Timothy 2:15, 3:16; Romans 2:28-29; Philippians 2:9-11; Isaiah 45:22-23; Revelation 2:5; Isaiah 56:5; Hebrews 12:22; Revelation 21:1-5

The Church at Laodicea . . . Colossians 3:3; 2 Corinthians 5:17; Luke 9:23; Romans 12:1-2 1; John 2:22-23; 1 John 4:1-3; 2 Timothy 4:2-4; Matthew 19:21; Luke 14:33; Hebrews 10:25

Chapter 4

Revelation 4: 1-11

The letters to the churches left John speechless. He could offer nothing further about the age of the church. With the end of the letter to Laodicea, John no longer mentions the Church at all in his vision from heaven. The fourth chapter of the "Revelation" moves from the Church on earth to the throne room of God in heaven. Except for his closing, John has no further need even for the word "Church." John realized that the Church under that title has ceased to exist with the change of scene. The Church is now the bride of Christ represented by twenty-four elders around the throne of God. At the end of the age of the lukewarm Church, the Church will be raptured, moved to heaven where wonderful occurences will take place.

How can we be sure this is what John was seeing? Several indications come from John himself. Christ had already told him in the letter to the church at Philadelphia that the true Church would not suffer the tribulation. The fourth chapter starts with the phrase "After this." John was indicating that after this last part of the age of the Church, it moves to heaven. And John's refusal to use the term Church denotes that change.

The true Church will be raptured. There is a false church, a huge number of professing Christians who have not repented and in reality been saved. This church will continue on earth for at least a short period of time during the tribulation. It is sad to think that some churches' only indication that the rapture has occurred will be the news on television.

The rapture of the Church will start into motion events in heaven that will lead to the tribulation. It will also change some relationships for believers in heaven. John no longer refers to God as a "Father" from this point on. God is now referred to in terms of holiness, almighty power, and Lord. God's position has changed. He has been the Heavenly Father, providing for His children. Now His children are with Him, and He is taking the position that so many people think of Him in now, a powerful, thundering judge of the righteous and unrighteous, giving His power to His Son who has earned the right to be Judge of all.

John did not give us the signs to look for before the rapture. He was familiar with the various prophecies already given by divine inspiration from the writings of Daniel, Isaiah, Zechariah, and others in the old writings of Judaism. He was also familiar with what he and others had recalled and recorded about what Christ had said must happen at the time of the rapture and tribulation. John was not inspired to write down these matters again. But through his mind undoubtedly passed the signs of the times.

Israel would become a nation again in its own land with Jerusalem as its capital. Its rise to national independence would bring a rise of many enemies trying to snatch the land away. The Roman Empire would come to life stronger than before. Mystery religions and the occult, including numerology, astrology, belief in reincarnation, and open Satanism, would increase dramatically. They would be disguised as the "New Age" movement. There would be an increase in the use of drugs and alcohol, along with a rise in crime, war, natural and man-made disasters, diseases with no cures, pollution, and immorality. While these horrors accelerate true church involvement, meaningful worship, and the importance of the family unit would decline. These were just several of the signs given in Scripture as portents of the coming time of the tribulation. John, of course, did not know that 1900 years later, at the end of the twentieth century, most of these signs would be obvious.

As John recorded what he was seeing, he reminded himself and those who would read what he recorded, that it was all real. He was going through those experiences firsthand through the intervention of the Holy Spirit.

As he winged spiritually up to heaven he saw its outer door opened. It had been opened many years before by the victory over sin and death won by Christ on the cross and in the tomb. Because of Christ, the door had already been opened for John to look into heaven and for those who believe in Him to enter heaven when they leave this earthly life.

As he entered through the door, John heard a voice he recognized as that of Christ – the "voice" of a trumpet calling for the assembling of His followers and asking John to view for himself the inner court of God.

With the Spirit continuing to lead and guide him John found himself in that inner throne room, the place of the rule of God. On the throne He could only make out the glory of God. It was so bright, like a thousand lasers through precious gems, that he could not distinguish anything but the holy aura. God was on His throne, yet Christ was not at His right hand. John recognized that meant the age of grace had passed, and the judgment of God was at hand.

Around the throne was an unusual rainbow, not a multicolored arch like John had seen so many times in the sky, but a complete circle surrounding the throne. The circle was entirely the color of bright emeralds, a royal green. The circle of green meant that God was at the center of eternal life. The fact that it was equated to a rainbow was a reminder to John that God never forgets His promises to man. Noah had that same promise. All of God's promises would be remembered. Even in His judgment there would be grace to those who believed.

Outside of this circle of green were twenty-four elders, representing the tribes of Israel and the Apostles of the Church. They stand for the true Church itself. John recognized them as the Church because of the white robes they wore, a robe Christ had promised him one day. On their heads were crowns, rewards for faithful service under Christ's Lordship. The crowns of those of the Church were alike, yet each different. Some wore crowns of life, having been martyred for their faith. Some wore crowns of righteousness, having eagerly watched and waited for the events that had culminated in the rapture. Some wore crowns of proclamation, having truthfully and unashamedly proclaimed through preaching, teaching, personal witnessing, song, and writings the glorious Gospel of Christ, including the warnings to those who refused to believe. Some wore crowns of glory for having ministered in His name. All wore the basic crown of victory, the incorruptible crown given to all who sincerely believe.

As John observed the scene, from the throne God spoke and His voice was like thunder and lightning, and the sound of multitudinous other voices. God's voice of thunder and lightning always precedes His coming storm of judgment.

In front of the throne was the Holy Spirit showing Himself as seven flaming torches. The presence of the Spirit and the elders with their crowns meant that the church had not only been raptured, but each individual had stood before God and received his reward. Some had their works destroyed because they were not Godly. Others had their works rewarded. God had observed all their works. His clear knowledge of those works was shown by the presence of a sea of crystal in front of His throne. The sea was as smooth as glass, with not even a ripple to disturb its surface. For the church this meant that not only had the individuals of the Church been justly rewarded, but now the Church was at peace. There would be no more worldly turmoil for it.

What John beheld next brought to his mind's eye the prophecies of Ezekiel and Isaiah. Around the throne of God, at four strategic points were four creatures, standing guard and ready to do God's will. As John tried to describe them, he knew they were the royal seraphim and cherubim, special angelic-type creatures whose image had been on the lid of the ark of the covenant. Their many eyes showed they were constantly alert and watching. Their multi-wings revealed their ability to move powerfully and quickly in any direction. The fact that there were four of them with different faces had, in John's thoughts, two meanings. The lion, the man, the ox, and the eagle were the four staff symbols for the marching standards of Israel used especially during the period of the Exodus. Behind each of these standards had marched a section of three tribes. These creatures stood as special messengers and guardians of God's followers.

These four creatures also had the faces of each Gospel story. John's companion, Matthew, had already written the story of Christ, showing Him to be the King of Israel, the Lion who rules. Mark, with the obvious help of Peter, had recorded the earthly ministry of Christ, showing Him as a suffering servant, the Ox who bears the burden. The physician Luke, after many hours of personal interviews with Mary, Jesus' half-brothers and sisters, and many others, had written the life of Christ as a man. John himself had recently added his memories, filling in many blanks left by the others. John had tried to show the Deity and majesty of Christ. The eagle was the creature of Deity and majesty.

While vigilant, these four creatures were also leading the worship of God. Their proclamations call for all of creation to worship the only true God. When they call for worship, all present around the throne join in.

As John's observations continued, he saw pure worship occur for the first time. He had seen the ceremonies of the Temple in Jerusalem. He had led in mighty revival services, with glorious music and a multitude of decisions for Christ. He had experienced firsthand the direct outpouring of the Holy Spirit. But all of these were but foggy attempts at the true, pure worship he now saw. The creatures initiated it, and immediately all those surrounding the throne joined in.

The elders cast their crowns at the base of the throne. All they had, all they were was because God so loved them He gave His Son to pay the price of their sins (see John 3:16). That payment had elevated them to God's family and heirs. When worship started, they realized they deserved none of this and gave willingly and lovingly their rewards and privileges back to Him. He would return them in love.

John recognized that these believers had finally achieved their created purpose. Man, who God created as a special creature of love, worship, and direct fellowship, had willfully and purposely broken that relation by sin, starting in the Garden of Eden. Now, man through faith in God's Son had been restored. This was what God had intended all along—worship, fellowship, and love directly with God.

The Church down through history would constantly need to be reminded of man's purpose. Churches would forget the *why* of worship and concentrate only on the *how*. In the process they would inhibit worship and never really experience it. How many churches today claim worship, but only have ceremony?

As John marveled at the sights and sounds of adoration, he wondered how many people with whom he had talked would end up in this worship experience. His revelation of this worship experience would challenge us to look closely at the attempts to worship in the church from his time to ours. His vision still challenges the church to ask what it is doing and why. It challenges the individual to ask himself why he desires to go to heaven. Many would answer that question by saying that they do not want to go to hell, but the real reason for desiring to go to heaven reaches far beyond a fear of hell. It should be rooted in a deep, soul-felt desire to truly worship and be with the God who created, redeemed, and loved us.

References:

1 Corinthians 15:51; 1 Thessalonians 4:16-17; John 10:9; Psalm 11:4; 1 Chronicles 24; Revelation 21:12-14; 2 Corinthians 5:21; 1 Corinthians 6:3; 1 Thessalonians 2:19; 2 Timothy 4:8; Philippians 4:1; James 1:12; 1 Peter 5:4; 1 Corinthians 9:22; 1 John 2:28; 1 Corinthians 3:14-15; 2 John 8; Exodus 25; Ezekiel 1:5-14, 10:9-16; Isaiah 6:2-3

Chapter 5

Revelation 5: 1-14

The former church and heavenly chorus had demonstrated true worship in John's presence. He had seen the presence of God and His Spirit, but missing from the scene was one John loved dearly, the *Son of God.* His absence from His position at God's right hand was disturbing. But before John could dwell on that his attention was drawn back to the throne.

Now he could make out the right hand of God and in it a tightly rolled document in the form of a scroll. It was sealed with seven seals. Roman law dictated that a last will and testament of a person had to have seven seals. Each seal could be broken only by someone authorized by that document. It might be seven individual people, each one authorized to break only one seal and roll the scroll out to its next seal. It might be one person, given all authority. Hebrew law required the title deed of a person's property, if sold to pay debts, to be sealed with seven seals. If a family member or someone willing to pay the entire price to redeem the property for the family paid the debt, then that person was authorized to open the seals and return the deed to its original owner.

This scroll represented to John both the final will of God for man and the title deed to all creation. Contained in it would be God's perfect destiny for mankind. When it was opened God's dominion and justice would be revealed. Man had sold this world to Satan for the mere pittance of a moment of sin. Satan, until Christ, held the deed to man and creation. Christ paid the price to redeem man and creation and now would have the right to open the seals and return the deed to its original owner, God. But where was Christ? John could not see Him.

One of God's higher-ranking angels broke into John's thoughts again, making a challenge to find who might be worthy to take the scroll of ultimate destiny and title. But no one could be found who had that authority, that right, and that power. For a moment John sensed terror that caused him to weep. If no one could be found, what would happen to the believers, to creation and to the kingdom Christ had told him about during their brief time together on earth? He had not felt like this since that day he had watched Christ die on the cross. Waves of helplessness had almost overcome him that day, and now those overcoming waves rose up again.

With compassion one of the elders reached out to John. His words of reassurance started with a description of One who was worthy to receive the scroll and open all seven seals. He was the Lion of Judah. John was aware the tribe of Judah had been told from the days of Jacob that it would be the ruling tribe of God's people. The Lion of this tribe would be the promised King of kings and Lord of lords, the Messiah. The elder continued in his description of the One who was worthy. He was the Root of David. This was a reminder to John that David, the greatest king of Israel, had been promised that from his family tree would spring this same Messiah who would rule a kingdom of the entire world.

At the instant the elder finished his comforting description, John noticed that between them and the throne stood a familiar figure. The recollections of Judah and Israel cause John to describe this figure in extremely special terms. He was the little baby lamb that had been slain but was alive.

John was recalling the Passover lamb. For Jewish boys the Passover had been special, but in many ways difficult. A requirement of Passover was to adopt a small lamb, perfect in every way, and let it come into the house to live for many days. That lamb became the family pet, and John had even named them when he was a little boy. But on the night of Passover the family was required to kill the family pet. It brought into focus the real meaning of sacrifice. It was so painful to kill the little innocent life they had grown to love and considered a part of the family.

John could not help but describe his beloved Christ in the terms of this little lamb. What love there had been for Him, the most perfect from His Heavenly Father. How difficult it had been to see Him killed, an innocent life for so many who were so filthy in sin. He had been sacrificed, not merely for the people who lived when He lived on this earth. He had been sacrificed with full knowledge of each individual who would be born from then until the end of time. That knowledge included a complete realization of all the sins that each person would commit. Yet this Lamb still willingly gave Himself for each person.

He paid the price for all sin on the cross and defeated the power of sin there. But the "Lamb" that John beheld was alive. The price Christ paid was not just to defeat sin, but was also to defeat death. His being alive with the multitude of believers there in the throne room lifted John to greater heights of joy than he had ever experienced before.

Here was the Son of God, with all power (seven horns), all knowledge (seven eyes) and the fullness of the Spirit of God. The One John had seen rejected, despised, mocked, laughed at, and crucified was now about to assume what was rightfully His.

From the right hand of God, Christ took the scroll. He had earned the right and privilege of this moment. Only He had been completely man and yet completely sinless. Only He had conquered sin and death. Only in Him could man ever have any hope of eternal life with God.

At the moment Christ took the scroll, worship on a new scale started. Led by the four creatures around the throne and the believers, led by the twenty-four elders, John was aware of music and prayers of praise that had been building for thousands of years. As he watched he saw all the prayers answered of all the believers and people of faith of all time. The desire for an end to Satan's war against man, the termination of the results of sin, and the establishment of the Kingdom of the Lord was about to be granted.

The worship that John recorded was unlike any seen on earth. Those participating sang a new song. The old songs were about the "Lamb" of God. The new song was about the "Lion" of God. The time of grace and the intercession of Christ had come to an end. The time of judgment and the rule of Christ was imminent. And as John watched he became aware of the vast multitude of the heavenly host singing praises to God and to His Son. Only He is Worthy! Only He is in control! Only He is Salvation! Only He is King!

References:

Zechariah 5:1-3; John 15:15; Genesis 49:9-10; 2 Samuel 7; 1 Chronicles 17:11-14; Isaiah 9:6-7; John 1:29; Isaiah 58:6-7; Exodus 12; Daniel 7–8; John 16:33; Romans 8:34-37

Chapter 6

Revelation 6: 1-17

The chorus of heavenly worship ended, and Jesus is about to start opening the scroll sealed with seven seals. John's attention was directed by an angel to watch from his heavenly reviewing stand the events of a history yet to be. It would be a time of horror on such an unprecedented scale that even 1,900 years later men would have difficulty comprehending it all.

What John was about to see would be the time prophesied by Daniel and Jesus, the period of the tribulation. These prophecies predicted that the tribulation would last seven years. In it man's sin would be allowed to reap completely what it had sown. Until the time that the tribulation started, John recalled that Christ had promised the Holy Spirit would keep evil from running totally wild. But during the tribulation, the controlling influence of God's Spirit would be removed from the earth. The Spirit would still work in individual lives, but only on the same scale as Old Testament prophets had seen. The outpouring of the Spirit experienced during the age of the Church would be no more. Only individuals would feel, sense, and believe.

Daniel had prophesied that this final seven years would be broken in half. For the first half there would be one of power who would deceive Israel and make that nation think he was its friend. During the tribulation—evil, immorality, war, famine, disease and disaster on a worldwide scale would be rampant. After the first half of the tribulation, the one of power would reveal himself as being the exact opposite of Christ, and would be fully empowered by Satan to try to destroy the authentic believers of Israel and anyone else who in truth followed God.

This seven-year period would be ushered in with the rapture of the Church. This event would create such confusion, it would allow the up-and-coming Antichrist to consolidate his power and work to control all the world. He would promise peace but deliver war. He would promise a time of plenty for all but would deliver this abundance to those who worshiped him alone.

All others would face torture, persecution, and death. He would claim he was from God, the Messiah, even God incarnate. He would have power to deceive the majority of people, and they would follow like pigs to the slaughter house. Evil would reign. Comparatively few would be saved. Judgment from Christ will come. This seven-year period will be the last chance for Israel to repent and return to God. It will be all of mankind's final opportunity to believe. Tragically, many will not take this opportunity. John fully understood this prophecy. Now his angelic guide instructed him to watch as Christ opened the sealed scroll.

The first seal was broken, and an order went out from Christ to allow the first of four horsemen to move over the earth. It was a white horse. The rider was the deceiver, the coming Antichrist. The horse he rode was one of conquering, and on it the rider would grab control of the world. The rider promises peace and for a moment, if John had not looked closely, he might have thought that this was Christ coming to set up His kingdom. But Christ was there in heaven, and the peace this rider promised lasted only for a very short period of time. Like others before him, this rider was canny enough to realize to attract followers you have to promise peace, even peace at any price. Many leaders before him will have tried to guarantee peace, even if it meant war. But this rider is the smartest of them all, and his promise of peace would still be broken.

The rider had a bow in his hand. A bow is an instrument of war, but not Christ's instrument. Whenever Christ had referred to an instrument of war He would use, it was always a two-edged sword. A bow is only part of a weapon. It is the part that controls a missile, the launching mechanism of a tool of death. This rider would come to control the weapons of war for the entire world. Whether they were to be slingshots or weapons about which John had no concept – nuclear bombs – he would have all in his control.

He had been given a crown which *he had placed on his own head.* He crowned himself. He had not earned this crown as Christ had. It was given to him. And it was not even a permanent crown. This crown was one similar to those laurel-wreath crowns given at Olympic games, a temporary crown that would soon be destroyed.

This rider was the Antichrist rising to power. It would be three-and-one-half years before he would be totally indwelt by Satan, but during that interim period he would still do intense harm.

The white horse had appeared only for a short period of time when Christ broke the second seal and gave the order for the next horse and rider to move over the earth. This horse was red, the red of blood shed in war and violence. His coming would expose the first rider's promises to be a lie, but the deception of the first rider was already ingrained, and people would follow him all the more. War, true worldwide war, would be willingly fought because the leader of the world would lie and argue it was his means of keeping the peace.

The rider of the second horse carried the sword of an assassin. John had seen this sword used before by bigoted people intent on wiping out entire races of people in the name of justice and humanity. It was the sword of legalized murder to further promote the position of the Antichrist. History would see this sword used many times. Even the supposed followers of Christ would use it in inquisitions and "holy" wars. Races in power would use it to enslave other races. Nations led by demon-possessed leaders would employ it to create holocausts. Rapidly this horse moved across the time of history, and Christ opened the third seal.

An order came to let the third horse and rider move out. This horse was black, the horse of universal famine. Famine usually follows war, especially for the losers of the war. This is famine more intense than ever before seen. It is famine when there is still food to feed the hungry. The rider of this horse carries a scale. The price of one meal would cost a person an entire day's pay. If a person has to work all day just to feed himself, what will happen to his family and those who depend on him to provide food, clothing, and shelter? While some struggle to find food, others who are supporters of the Antichrist will be having steak, caviar, lobster, and all the trimmings. They will be riding in limousines, living in mansions, and thinking they have arrived in Utopia.

The rider holding the scales revealed to John that the person who decided who would eat and who would not would be the leader, the rising Antichrist. Physical survival would depend on the individual's loyalty to this false savior.

The tragedy of the first three riders was great. Then Christ opened the fourth seal and commanded the last horse and rider to go. It was a pale horse, the horse of pestilence, disease, and death. Riding with this last rider was the second death, the final, eternal separation from God in torment forever. John viewed diseases he did not know existed, diseases that could not be cured and that spread epidemically – super viruses would exist, diseases of the blood that would break down a person's ability to resist even the simplest of illnesses to cure. Even if there were cures, the struggle to survive would eliminate any possibility of being able to afford the cure.

The death this rider ushered in was extensive. It was spread by disease-carrying animals and crazed gangs of violent humans. John could not see how many died but was informed by his angelic guide that one quarter of all who lived at that time would perish. (Nineteen-hundred years later the population of the world would be over five billion people.) The tribulation had just started, and over one in four people were dead! Some of those who died had become believers in Christ. They had been persecuted for not supporting the rising Antichrist and had died of starvation, torture, or murder. Christ now opened the fifth seal, and it revealed what had been happening to these tribulation saints. At the altar of prayer in heaven John saw the tribulation saints and their prayers being heard by Christ. The response to those prayers was Christ's personal promise of justice that would come in a short period of time. When that justice came, these saints would be vindicated and their tormentors judged for eternity.

For some John recognized there was hope affirmed by faith in Christ. These would be the believers or saints of the tribulation. With all the war, famine, disease, and death he had witnessed, he needed to share hope with those who would read this revelation.

Then Christ opened the sixth seal. Instantly the entire earth shook. The impact of this seal's being broken was not just on the earth. The sun was blackened and the moon turned red. Stars fell from the sky in a shower of light. The very atmosphere of the earth was torn in two, and the land masses moved from their foundations. Nature and the universe were in turmoil, a result of thousands of years of man's sin.

What caused the sun to darken and the moon to look like blood? John could not tell, but it appeared that the atmosphere had become clouded with all sorts of debris, smoke, and soot, possibly from the wars that continued to be fought.

Whatever the cause of this turmoil, whether it was war that used the power of the sun or nature's simple reacting to man's rebellion against God, the intensity was so great that every living person sought shelter. Their fears were so dreadful they prayed to anything and anyone to provide shelter from this nightmare. They called and prayed to everyone but God. Even in this time of death and disaster, they refused to place their lives into His hands by faith. They wanted the wrath of the Lamb to end. It was a strange statement for John to record the "wrath of the Lamb." Lambs are not creatures of wrath, anger, or violence. They are meek, mild, and lovable. But the Lamb being talked about here was not any lamb. This was the Lamb of God, Jesus Christ.

John had seen the wrath of this Lamb before. He had watched while Christ had driven the wealthiest and most powerful men of Jerusalem out of the Temple because they were making a profit at the expense of God and His worship. Those powerful men then had not been able to stand against the Lamb's wrath. John had seen it again as Christ went to a fig tree that should have had ripe, juicy, sweet figs on it. Instead Christ found that this tree had no fruit at all. He cursed it, and it immediately withered and died. This was but a sampling of the wrath of the Lamb to come, a wrath that John now perceived clearly. The time of the meek and lowly Lamb of God had ended. Now He would set things straight and put each individual in his rightful place for eternity.

It was a horrible scene John witnessed. People who would read it through the years would be challenged by it. The question of being truly saved and committed should be asked of every person who would read these first events in the first half of the tribulation. John was asking all who read his writings, "Are you absolutely sure you are a true believer in Jesus Christ as your Savior and Lord? Are you demonstrating that your life belongs to Him by bringing forth the fruits of repentance and salvation? If you do not know what those are, maybe you do not know the One who provides them."

References:

Matthew 24:4-31; Daniel 9:24-27; Lamentations 4:8-9; Luke 11:50-51; Nahum 1:5; Romans 1:18; John 2:15-17; Matthew 21:12-16; Mark 11:21

Chapter 7

Revelation 7: 1-17

John had watched as Christ had broken six of the seven seals on the title deed and will of God. The destruction, death, pain, and horror even he could not put into adequate words. The fifth seal had shown the souls of some who had become honest-to-goodness believers during this time. John wondered about these believers. Who were they? How did they come to the faith? What would happen to them with the restraining power of the Holy Spirit having been removed?

Christ paused in His authorization of the continuation of the time of tribulation to provide answers to John's unspoken questions. These answers were words of reassurance to John and to the following generations that those who have faith in Christ will be saved.

Four angels could now be seen, standing at opposite poles and positions of the earth. To them had been given the power to destroy life in the sea and life coming from the earth. Their power of destruction was given by Christ himself, but before they began their tasks, another powerful angel intervened. Carrying the official seal of the Kingdom of the Lord, he mandated that these four angels delay their release of judgment until those who really believed might be marked with the seal.

John was conversant with the sealing of God through the Holy Spirit. He had experienced it personally the day he believed in Jesus Christ as Savior and Lord. Each genuine believer was sealed by the Holy Spirit, a sealing to show who owned them, who had paid the price for them. Believers have always needed to be sealed. There has never been a believer that could maintain his own salvation. John knew that even after he was saved, he had sinned, but the sealing of the Spirit became a quick conscience that haunted him until he honestly repented of the sin.

Sealing has been a part of God's grace ever since that grace became incarnate. Sealing was not only designed to insure salvation, it was given as an empowering agent so that each believer in each generation might serve God. There has never been a true preacher, teacher, minister, deacon, or other servant of God that has not been sealed. Sealing shows ownership, loyalty, dominion, and authority. What John noted was a special sealing's taking place. The believers at the time of the tribulation would need a physical presence to help remind them of the spiritual power they still had. The persecution, destruction, pain, terror, and sacrifices they would have to suffer would mandate a special mark that would reassure them and testify to others.

The angel moved forward to seal one specific group of believers. As John watched, the angel identified 12,000 members of each tribe of the nation of Israel who had become believers. The total sealed from Israel would be 144,000. These would make up a special envoy of powerful evangelists proclaiming Jesus as the true Messiah. They would witness to the entire world, filling an ecclesiastical void left by the rapture of the church.

Israel was honored with the special sealing as it had always been honored by God. The promises of God to Abraham, Isaac, and Jacob, along with the promises to David and the other leaders of Israel, would always be remembered by God. For His chosen people, Israel, He would always have a special place of service. The nation He had chosen thousands of years before to bring forth the Messiah and to proclaim the good news of God would also have a signal place during the tribulation. A small portion who finally understood God's Word would be sealed for salvation and service. But it would not be at all easy. This sealing would bring additional hardship, persecution, and death to their followers. It would cost them, even their lives, to follow Jesus.

As the names of the tribes were called out for the sealing of their believers, John recorded that Judah was first. Reuben had been the firstborn of Jacob and should have been listed first. But Reuben had lived in sin and lost its reward and honor. John knew of Christians who would suffer similarly. Because they continued to live in sin they would lose their reward and honor. They would be saved, but not rewarded as God had initially desired (see 1 Cor. 3:10-15).

John also pointed out that two of the tribes of Israel, Dan and Ephraim, were totally omitted. Dan was not sealed because Dan had led, in the past, in the worship of other gods. Dan was the tribe that had been foretold as bringing additional trouble to Israel during the time of the tribulation. Some even believed that from Dan would come one of the Antichrist's strongest followers and supporters. It was too gross to consider, a member of the chosen people of God supporting the enemy of God.

Ephraim was also omitted. Ephraim not only worshiped other gods, but also had led in the division of the Kingdom of Israel that David and Solomon had finally consolidated. There was a price to be paid for any person or group of people who divided any part of God's family. How John hoped that message would finally sink in with the many churches he knew of that were constantly fighting among themselves!

The believing portion of the nation of Israel had its special sealing. Then John reported that a large number of Gentiles also were sealed. This sealing was similar to that of the 144,000. They were sealed for salvation and service, but they would be led in that service by the 144,000. John could not number the Gentiles by himself. Had he had time, and others there with him to assist in the counting, the number could have been tabulated. But numbers were not as important as God's Word to every man to make sure that they would be among those who were sealed, preferably before the rapture of the church.

John was fully aware that during the tribulation there would be no "secret Christians." The marks they would have, both physically and spiritually, would be evident to all they encountered. Those marks would be a testimony of faith and evidence that would invite persecution on them from the Antichrist.

As John continued to watch, he sat in on another type of worship experience. It was led by a group of believers John had not seen assembled before. He recognized they were believers, for they had received their robes of righteousness, showing they had been cleansed by the sacrifice of Christ.

This time the worship reminded John of the day that Christ had ridden into Jerusalem on a colt. The Church had called it His "triumphal entry" into Jerusalem, but that entry had ending in His crucifixion. It was more of a *victorious exit* than a triumphal entry. John now viewed a new type of triumphal entry, with the waving of the palm branches of victory and peace. These saints now celebrated their triumph – a triumph made possible only by their personal faith in Jesus Christ as their Savior and Lord.

Their songs and shouts of praise echoed across heaven. What had appeared to unbelievers as defeat on earth was victory in heaven. Their faith had been affirmed. Their hope had been honored. Their eternal life had only just begun.

John was confused. He was asked by an elder standing nearby if he could identify those saints. John neither knew them nor could identify them. They appeared like members of the Church, but they were not. These were some new type of believer.

The elder quickly explained to John that these were believers, saints, who had given their lives for the faith during the tribulation. They were not in their resurrected bodies as yet. They would not be given those until later, but their spirits, their souls, were present with the Lord because their bodies had been slain. They represented those already slain and those that would be murdered during the remaining time of the tribulation. These special saints were now rejoicing. The hunger and thirst they had experienced physically under the repressive rule of the Antichrist would be no more. The inflicted pain, oppression, and heat of trials would be no more. They were now released from the bondage of sin and the resulting tribulation.

As the worship continued, John had been given this brief glimpse back into heaven to provide a renewal of hope. The tribulation had just begun. It would soon intensify with the breaking of the seventh seal, followed by the sounding of seven trumpets and the pouring out of seven bowls of wrath. These would multiply the outrages already seen. It is always comforting to know that God is still in control. He would never forget those on earth who confessed their faith in Him. He would never forgive those who finally refused to make that confession. How He wanted to tell the world to repent and believe. Maybe they would repent and believe when they read what Christ revealed to John. Maybe, but he knew in the back of his mind many would continue to make excuses, laugh, and deny who Christ is.

References:

Psalm 148:8; 2 Corinthians 1:22, 5:5; Ephesians 1:13-14, 4:30; Romans 11; Matthew 25:31-46; Judges 18:30; Genesis 49:17; 1 Kings 11:26; John 12:12-13

Chapter 8

Revelation 8: 1-13

Christ broke the seventh seal. Suddenly there was complete silence throughout heaven. It was such a stark contrast to the events immediately preceding, that automatically everyone's attention was turned to the Lamb. For a brief moment in history even God contemplated what was happening. Even God, who loved His creation called man so much that He sent His Son to die for them, stopped to allow the full depth of what was about to happen to be understood. In that brief silence, those on earth who had refused to believe had another chance to turn from their wickedness to life in Christ. But few accepted the opportunity.

John's attention was now drawn to seven angels holding seven trumpets. These were the trumpets calling the next events to attention and duty; seven trumpets trying to get man's attention and declaring the ultimate return of the King and His Kingdom. That return would bring additional judgment, just like the trumpet blasts that had reverberated off the walls of the fortress town of Jericho. As each angel sounded, other types of walls would crumble, and those who stood in the way of Christ's taking what had always been His would be buried in the rubble.

As these angels prepared to blow the call of Christ to history, John looked at another angel taking incense and placing it on the altar of prayer. Christ was now ready to answer the prayers of all the saints for justice. Those who had been hindered, abused, neglected, persecuted, or murdered would now be vindicated. Those who rejected Christ through obvious outward actions or who simply rejected Him through neglect would shortly answer for the actions and attitudes of their earthly lives.

The prayers of the saints were answered with the fires of judgment on Christ rejecters. These fires had rained down on earth before at Sodom and Gomorrah, and for Elijah when pursued by soldiers of the king as he contested the religion of the prophets of Baal. Throughout the story of God and His love there had been fires of judgment—answers to Godly people's prayers for a demonstration of God and His perfect character.

As the fire rained down toward earth, the multi-voices of God Himself were heard giving direction and purpose to this coming judgment. John stood in awe as the presence and involvement of God were emphasized by thunder, lightning, and earthquakes. These were signs God had used many times to Israel to reveal His presence, power, and authority. At Sinai, during the wilderness wanderings, to the prophets, and even at a hill called Calvary, these signs had shown God being involved with every phase of what was happening.

When the prayers were heard and answered, the seven angels came to attention and prepared to sound the notes of God's will. The first angel sounded, and immediately across the earth one-third of the greenery was destroyed with a fiery hailstorm. With famines already present, and the atmosphere already polluted, people now faced less food and less oxygen because the plants that cleaned the air naturally were gone. More disaster occurred through the rich soil's being blown or washed away, for there was no longer the root system to hold it in place. There was now not enough food to sustain animal life. Meat from cattle, farm animals, and wild game became a rarity.

John had a glimpse of what had happened to the Pharaoh of Egypt when he refused to let Israel go. What John witnessed now was a repeat of the seventh plague on Egypt—the falling of disastrous hail—but this was on a worldwide scale. God was acting against His third day of creation when He had created plant life, judging what He had called "good" then, as now being infected by man's sin. Paul had expressed it well to the Romans in a letter John had been heard about years before. All of creation groans because of the sin of man (see Rom. 8:22).

The second angel brought his trumpet to his lips and blew the second notes of God's will. The echoes of the notes had not ended when an object that looked like a massive burning mountain fell into the waters of the world, and one-third of all the seas became blood. John could not identify exactly what this mountain was. It could have been a meteor from space or a manmade type of destruction that had now been launched and used against mankind and creation. It may even have been the result of a series of sub-oceanic volcanic eruptions, but whatever it was, God had ordained it. Sea life in the afflicted areas died, and the ships that sailed those seas, whether military, commercial, or pleasure were destroyed.

The famine had been increased. The seafood industry was all but destroyed. The ability of commerce to distribute food and manufactured goods to markets and places of need around the world had been drastically reduced—and the tools of war to stop invading armies at the shores of many countries were now rusting at the bottom of the oceans.

It was another glimpse of the plagues against Pharaoh, the first plague that had turned the Nile into blood. Now the world had an idea that what this plague had been like. It was also God's judgment of His fifth day of creation when He had brought forth life in the sea and birds in the air; these too had become diseased by man's sin.

The third trumpet sounded, and John watched as a star fell out of the sky onto the earth and polluted one-third of the fresh water. The effects of this was similar to the seas being turned into blood. There was a shortage of water, not only for humans, but for all creation. Fish, water fowl, and domestic and wild animals now died, either from the lack of water or from drinking the poisoned water. Men became crazy with thirst and drank the poisoned water, realizing it would cause a tortuous death.

The star that caused this, John could identify as "Wormwood." It was a name that indicated to Israel that its calamity was due to worshiping idols. The idols Israel had worshiped had been more than little statues and figurines. Israel had come to know that the name "Wormwood" meant any person, place, or thing that was put in place of God, that removed God from being first in every part of their lives.

Three angels had sounded their trumpet blasts, bringing three calamities that had destroyed one-third of the prospective targets. Now the fourth angel raised his trumpet, and the blast triggered the immediate loss of one-third of the light of the sun, moon, and stars. With one-third less light, there would be one-third less time for crops to grow and one-third less security. The lessening of light could also mean a dramatic decrease in the quality of the atmosphere as plants would have less time to cleanse the air. Air pollution on a scale larger than believed possible could block out the light of the sun itself. There would be one-third less of a chance of recovery from the first three trumpet blasts.

John no doubt saw that this judgment was similar to the ninth plague on Egypt, a darkness that covered the land with such oppression that if could be felt. It was also judgment aimed at the fourth day of creation when God provided light for man through the sun, moon, and stars.

The first four angels had sounded their calls of judgment. The four angels John had seen standing at the four corners of the earth before the sealing of the believers had each been released to destroy the section of the world over which they had been given authority. The winds of judgment had been released.

The toll of these first four blasts was staggering, especially when combined with the previous toll from the opening of the seals. War, famine, disease, pestilence, one-quarter of mankind killed, nature in turmoil, one-third of the vegetation, sea, fresh water, light, and possibly the atmosphere destroyed. John could not compute how many died from these individual judgments, but numerous people had perished from the drought, the disasters at sea, the drinking of the tainted water, and the breathing of a toxic atmosphere. Others had died in the terror and confusion of an entire world convulsed in sin.

What would the fifth trumpet signal? John could not imagine. As he tried to prepare himself for it, he spied another angel, soaring through the air like an eagle. From this winged messenger came the cry of warning to mankind. The first of three woes would come with the fifth trumpet. God was giving mankind another warning to repent. The seven broken seals and the first four trumpet blasts were nothing compared to what was about to happen!

References:

Psalm 141:2; Revelation 6:9-11; Exodus 9:23-24; Genesis 1; Jeremiah 51:25; Exodus 7:20-21; Psalm 105:29; Hosea 4:1-3; Deuteronomy 29:18; Jeremiah 9:13-15, 23:15; Lamentations 3:15,19; Matthew 24:29; Luke 21:25-26; Joel 2:10; Exodus 10:21-23

Chapter 9

Revelation 9: 1-21

John tried to prepare himself for the fifth trumpet. The warning of the coming woes by the angel also gave John the wisdom to anticipate that the events he was about to witness would involve more complex imagery, symbols, and ideas that would venture into a new level of the Spirit.

And he heard the fifth trumpet and watched as a star fell from heaven. This star was Satan, being allowed to release his demonic followers which had, in some cases, been imprisoned in the bottomless pit since the beginning of Satan's rebellion before time began. As John watched, Satan was given the key to that pit and with the opening of the pit, demons more horrible than man could ever imagine emerged to vent the pent-up rage of their imprisonment upon mankind.

John did not wish to identify these demons individually but recognized these beings as spiritual forces against God and His kingdom. Distorted by sin and rebellion, these had once been part of the heavenly host that had decided to follow Lucifer. From the time of the initial rebellion until now, some of them had been imprisoned by faith and prayer in this pit which John understood as the place of torment sometimes called hell. Others had been imprisoned throughout history. John remembered vividly one occassion near Gadara where he had encountered a man possessed by demons who called himself the name of "Legion." Now all these demons which had been imprisoned from before time to this point in the tribulation were being released.

The opening of the pit released the smoke and fire in which the creatures had been existing. The smoke created a darkness that actually teemed with evil. John was thankful that this darkness would not overcome the Light he knew. At the same time he wondered how any creature, especially man, could doubt the existence of an eternal place of torment, but he also knew, even with this further evidence, many would continue to deny any type of a hell.

With the world already in torment and chaos, with the multiple tragedies that had already occurred, now came a hellish host of evil personified. To John the only way he could describe these demonic beings was as mutant locusts. They were not normal in size, actions, or even appetite. They had stingers like scorpions, and that in itself must have made John shiver. He had felt that sting before. The wound had set his arm on fire, and the aftereffects had lasted almost half a year.

As John watched these "locusts" he noted that they attacked people; but not all people—only those who did not believe in Jesus. Believers were not being afflicted by the stings of these scorpions. As John marveled at this, suddenly he remembered, the believers had been sealed. These demons were inflicting pain on those who had not been protected. In much the same way as the Passover, when those who believed in God had spread the blood of the Passover lamb on the doorposts and lintels, and the angel of death had passed them by, the believers of the tribulation were passed over by the demons.

But those not protected by faith were being severely afflicted. The torment of these forces drove many to try to end their lives, but they could not kill themselves. Every attempt at suicide failed. There was no relief, no help, no hope. They had to endure the torment, and it lasted for five months. It was but a sampling of what these same unbelievers would endure for eternity in hell; everlasting torment with no way to find relief, not even death.

As John watched these demons, he was compelled to convey the power they had. They were like battle horses, large and wearing armor, making them difficult, if not impossible, to bring down. They had crowns of gold, earthly gold, showing they were beings of some authority and power. They had the faces of men, faces of intelligence, and a focused allegiance to complete their appointed tasks.

They had the hair of women. John had seen locusts before that had such long antennas that they looked like hair streaming back over their bodies. But these locusts had something more. Not only did this hair provide sensory perception to seek out and destroy or to move away to escape danger, this hair added an attractiveness to the beings, to deceive those they came to torture into drawing close to them.

Added to these attributes, these beings had the voracious appetite to devour their prey, even as a lion would. They had breastplates of iron to protect them from attack, to make them almost unstoppable. When they moved they sounded like the charge of horses and chariots that would elicit fear from the heart of the most courageous man.

But the two worst traits these creatures had were tails that could sting and torture and mouths that could inflict pain. The tails John had already identified as having the power to inflict the pain of a scorpion sting. The mouths, though, were a different matter. The pain inflicted by the mouths was not just a physical pain of biting. This pain was spiritual; these mouths inflicted their wounds by deceptive words that would deceive and lead many astray.

As John watched this host emerge and spread, he saw in their midst a leader, a king. Locusts in their natural state have no leaders or hierarchy. But these demonic creatures had as their leader a mighty demon, an archangel of Satan. His name in any language was destruction.

When the satanic forces were loosed and their mission of affliction was accomplished, John heard another warning from God's messenger, a warning of the coming of the second woe. With the warning came the blast of the sixth trumpet.

John's attention was focused on the altar of sacrifice in heaven, specifically on the horns of refuge of the altar. The laws of Israel stipulated that those guilty of certain crimes could seek refuge by clinging to these horns and would be probated by their actions of clinging to these horns. In heaven these horns signified those unjustly persecuted on earth for their faith in Christ. These were the horns of justice. From this area John hears the voice of Christ authorizing the release of four angels who have been bound in the area of the river named Euphrates.

John knew of these four angels who were powerful followers of Satan. They had been bound separate from the rest of the demonic forces because of their power. They had been bound in the area of the Euphrates River because this was the area of the first sin (Eve and Adam), the first murder (Cain and Abel), and the first earthly king who dared to assault heaven (Nimrod and the Tower of Babel). The Euphrates was also the Scriptural boundary of East and West. It had been from the time of Abraham the Eastern boundary of what the nation of Israel recognized as the Promised Land. The River Euphrates also flowed through Babylon, the center of sin and idolatry, the power base of Satan in the future.

These four angels had been bound and placed in this crossroads area of sin. Now they were about to be released, and their release would signal the preparation of an assault by the forces East of the river upon the land of promise, upon Israel itself.

As John viewed this release, he was reminded that this particular event had been in God's plan all along. God had foreknown the exact time these four would be freed and that the fury of these four would be released with them. Leading an army of 200 million men, these four would engineer a slaughter of one-third of mankind. Thus, the carnage they would execute would be staggering in numbers. John had a hard time imagining an army that size. He had no idea then that in 1,900 years an army of that size, and even larger, would exist in an area East of the Euphrates in a country that would be called China.

The four leaders of this army were powerful. Their power was shown not only in the horses they rode, but also in the armor they wore. The color of their standard was the red of fire and blood, judgment, and death; the blue of authority and leadership and the yellow of fear and slavery. They rode and controlled the horses of power, strength, and fear, horses that looked like lions and spit forth destruction like fire and brimstone. Even the tails of the horses they rode looked like snakes, inflicting pain with every flick. The destruction, the death, and the pain of mankind grew geometrically in front of John's eyes.

These four devilish generals and their army have added to the already incomprehensible toll. The numbers John remembered showed that, with the one-quarter of the population killed at the breaking of the fourth seal, the untold number who died when one-third of the oceans turned to blood, and one-third of the drinking water became poisoned, and now another one-third of the population wiped out, not counting those wounded, starving, diseased, tormented, and tortured, *over seven out of every twelve people who were living after the rapture of the church were dead!* They had all died in only three-and-one-half years.

John thought surely those surviving would now repent and turn to God. Certainly, after having gone through famines, wars, diseases, demonic assaults, torture, and what seemed like a thousand other trials and judgments, the survivors would see the truth and have it set them free. But the truth John was shown was contrary to the hopes he had.

Those who survived but did not believe refused to repent. Instead their sins increased. Their rebellion against God grew. All the areas God had shown He hated, they purposefully and willfully enhanced. The gods of materialism, pleasure, wealth, ego, and status were rededicated. The worship of the occult, even the worship of the very demons that had plagued them, grew.

John watched as four major sins clamped a vise-like grip on the surviving non-believers. In the streets around the world, murder, the use of drugs, witchcraft, sorcery, fortune telling, astronomy, sexual immorality, and robbery became the expected life-style. Their growth was insured because man's rebellion against God had reached its apex.

For a moment John had to remind himself that what he was watching was real. This was not a fictional play or an imaginative tragedy. This was what would happen in the future. He was not sure of the exact time these events would occur. He only realized that they would occur and that his commission from Christ was to record them accurately so all of God's children would know that, even in the horrible times of the tribulation, when evil seems to be totally out of control, God is still in charge. This reassurance to God's children would also, hopefully, testify to those outside of God's family about God's timetable of grace and love, along with His timetable of judgment and righteous wrath.

References:

Matthew 9:25-33; Matthew 8:28; Matthew 12:22; Mark 5:4; Mark 1:26-27; Luke 9:39; Matthew 10:8; Luke 4:41; Isaiah 14:12; Luke 10:18; 2 Corinthians 11:14; Ephesians 4:8-10; Matthew 12:40; 1 Peter 3:18-20; Luke 8:30ff; John 1:5; Joel 1 – 2; Jeremiah 8:3

Chapter 10

Revelation 10: 1-11

The horrors of the first six trumpets came to an end. John's attention was once again focused toward heaven. Descending in a cloud, clothed in the brightness of the sun and the colors of a rainbow, came an angel from the presence of God. His clothing reminded John that God was a God of covenant promises, like the promise of God to Noah shown in a rainbow. He was also a God of righteousness and purity shown in the dazzling appearance of this messenger. John had seen messengers like this before at the tomb of Jesus, after His resurrection. He had even seen his Savior with this glow of purity on the Mount of Transfiguration. The appearance then, as now, humbled John and caused a sense of peace and awe that some might even call fear.

The angel carried a small book, containing God's promises and provisions for man—promises and provisions that for the believer in Christ were reassuring, but for the unbeliever were condemning. The angel proclaimed with a voice like a roaring lion, the voice of authority, the Word of God. This Word was thunderous, revealing the innermost mind of God. As John started to write the revelation given in the resounding voice, he was suddenly commanded to keep secret this part of the Revelation. John understood the necessity for this secret and prayed that the readers of his letter would not try to supersede God's will by trying to guess what this secret was. John trusted God's wisdom and love, not only in the areas God wanted revealed, but especially in the areas that He knew were best kept secret.

This magnificent angel now took an oath to Christ, proclaiming on His authority that the end of time had arrived. John was relieved by this proclamation. He could not imagine how the earth could endure much more of the calamity and judgment it was now reaping. With his feet resting on land and sea, displaying his authority from God, the angel gave warning that the seventh and final trumpet would soon sound and that with its blast would come the revelation of God's final judgment, the filling of His wrath and the culmination of the time of tribulation.

Joined with these disclosures would be the divulgence of several of the deepest mysteries of God. Questions man has long asked would be answered, questions like, "Why do the innocent suffer?" "Why did God allow Satan to live to continually tempt man?" "Why does God love us and yet not force us to love Him?" These questions and many more would soon be answered. The prayers for justice would be answered, and the final validation of the prophetic words of God's servants through the ages would be given with them.

The angel turned to John and instructed him to take the book. The way the angel spoke, John was positive this was an authoritative request. The instructions given told John that he publicly had to request the book. God was allowing John a choice as to any further proclamation of His Word. John chose to take the book and requested the angel give it to him. As the angel handed John the book, he continued with special instructions for John. John was to eat the book. The angel was telling John to make God's Word a part of him. He was not merely to hear and see this revelation from God. He was not simply to relate it to others. He was to live, nourished by this Word. John was being recommissioned to go and tell, to teach and lead, to instruct and follow God's Word. The angel explained that this would not be easy. Parts of God's Word, especially what was being revealed to him now, were sweet. John was familar with those parts. He had written before the sweet words of God's love: "For God so loved the world that He gave . . ." How those words issued a rush of peace, joy, and happiness! God loves mankind that much. *How wonderful and marvelous is my God,* John reflected. But then the angel also declared that the Word of God would also be bitter.

This was the side of God's Word that John had a hard time stomaching. John was not the first preacher to have this problem. Jeremiah, Ezekiel, and even the writer of the Proverbs had known the bitter side of proclaiming God's Word. Yes, God loves the world, but He hates sin. Yes, God loves the sinner, but He cannot associate or even look upon him until he is cleansed by faith in Jesus. The bitter part of God's Word: for all who refused to believe, who never gave their life to Christ in faith, who never confessed, repented, and followed Him, there awaited judgment. That judgment clearly stated that man's works were inadequate. Man's sins, no matter how small and insignificant in man's sight, were gross in the eyes of God. Awaiting those who do not turn to God, God's Word promised eternal hell.

God recommissioned John. Tell the whole truth. There is the bitterness of sin or the sweetness of forgiveness. There is the bitterness of death or the sweetness of eternal life. There is the bitterness of righteous judgment or the sweetness of gracious salvation. There is the bitterness of eternal damnation in hell or the sweetness of eternal redemption in heaven. There is the bitterness of total devastation or the sweetness of a new creation. John comprehended both sides of God's Word. The angel with the little book had provided a pause for John to be recommissioned and reflect upon the urgency of his work. He was to tell the whole story. Not all would believe, but all would have to be told.

The angel ended his commissioning ceremony with a final note of encouragement. John must tell all mankind about Christ. He had written the Gospel story: now he would have to complete the Revelation. The Lamb of God that came to provide salvation is returning to judge those who refused His provision.

References:

Exodus 34:29; Luke 24:4; Matthew 17:1-2; Psalm 29; John 12:27-29; 2 Peter 3:9; Jeremiah 15:16; Ezekiel 3:1-3; Proverbs 16:24

Chapter 11

Revelation 11: 1-19

His recommissioning helped to prepare John for the seventh trumpet, but God wanted to show John something positive happening on earth in the midst of the tribulation. John was given a measuring rod and asked to measure the Holy Place of Worship, the central area of the Temple in Jerusalem. The Temple had been demolished when the Roman legions put down the rebellion of the zealots in 70 A.D. Being told to measure it indicated to John that someone had rebuilt the Temple. Sometime during the beginning of the tribulation Satan's chosen leader had made a deal with Israel and rebuilt the Temple.

Something had happened to the true worship of God in this structure supposedly dedicated to Him. Some type of desecration had been committed that necessitated God's meting out His justice. John was not given the details of these actions now. He simply moved to measure the area shown to him. His mind recalled other times when God instructed His leadership to use a measuring rod. Jeremiah had received similar instructions to measure those who in faith followed God and those who did not. The use of God's measuring rod was always a prelude to God's judgment.

John's instructions were to measure the place of worship and to leave out the areas along the fringe of worship. John was setting aside the bona fide believers, those who had finally turned back to God in faith and made a commitment based on that faith. John was to leave out those on the fringe, those who vacillated between believing God or following the world. Definitely left out of the measurement were those who refused to have spiritual contact with God. God had already measured these unbelievers and had found them falling short of God's requirement. They would have a short time of existence before God's measurements would culminate in His wrath and judgment.

In John's measurement he set aside the believers and saw for the first time two special leaders of the believers. John referred to them as "witnesses," a word he understood to mean one who would give his life to tell a message. The clearer meaning to John was "martyr." John noted that these two special witnesses were given three-and-one-half years to proclaim their message. It was a message that presented hope to the believers but persecution from those unbelievers. John remembered the little book he had just eaten and saw the sweet-and-bitter reality of God's message living in these two witnesses.

As John watched these two men, God told him these were the two representatives of the true Israel symbolized by Israel's official tree, the olive tree. They not only represented the genuine Israel, they shone light into a world darkened by sin. During this three-and-one-half-year period, evil would grow unabated. The Holy Spirit would not move to restrain the forces of evil as He had during the period of the Church. The world would need some message of good in this wicked environment. These two chosen men would lead in providing this message.

God would provide them special means with which to proclaim the truth. They would be able to call fire from heaven to destroy those who would try to stop them. They would be able to withhold rain from the most heavily laden clouds, to turn water into blood, and to strike both man and beast with plagues and diseases.

These abilities to perform miracles reminded John of men who had walked with God before. Elijah, the great prophet of God, and Moses, the great lawgiver of God, had possessed these powers. Could these be these two great men brought back to life on earth for this special mission? God had sent them back before to provide encouragement to Christ immediately before His crucifixion. John had seen them on the top of a mountain with

Christ and watched as their words aided in transfiguring the Messiah. This looked like the same men, but John did not dwell on that. It was sufficient that these were two special men, whether they be Elijah and Moses or two new lives.

God had given them unusual power and authority. At their will they could do miracles. They did not have to wait for further instructions from God. They had their task to perform, and they had the power with which to perform it. They set out to follow God. Oh, how John wished the members of the church could see these two and understand that God provides a task and the miraculous power to perform that task to each person who follows Him!

These two missionaries to a satanic world were invincible for three-and-one-half years. That was all God wanted from them. They proclaimed the truth of God to mankind. Some believed and followed, but most became agitated and turned against them. They were led by Satan's chosen leader. Their task done, God allowed these two to be taken by Satan's man. There was no trial. The verdict was pre-set. A swift, yet torturous, execution took place, and the people who hated them rejoiced that finally those two revival preachers were dead.

To make sure that everyone knew they were dead, to deflate the morale of the believers and to make fun of these two lives, their bodies were displayed for all the world to see. John had a hard time looking at this scene – these two who had given all, their bodies now made a grotesque centerpiece for a worldwide party. The party lasted three-and-one-half days. There was no doubt these two were dead. There was also no doubt that the majority of the world was happy to see them dead.

Then God intervened. With the whole world watching, suddenly God breathed life back into those dead, decaying bodies. It was a miracle to the unbelievers. To those who believed in God, it was God doing what He always has done, breathing life into those who die in Him. He had started that life in Eden, He had breathed new life into the faithful follower at a garden tomb outside of Jerusalem, near a place called Golgotha. He had continued to breathe new life—a new birth it was called—into every person who proclaimed Jesus as their personal Savior and Lord. Some might have called it a miracle. It was God showing His love once again.

With the breath of life in their bodies, the two witnesses stood up. The world gasped in horror and fear as they saw alive the ones they had killed. As they continued to watch, they heard a voice from heaven, and upon its command, the two men ascended into the clouds. John had watched Jesus leave the earth in much the same way. As they ascended, the earth began to shake and tremble. An earthquake, centered in Jerusalem, shook the bedrock of the world.

John had felt this same type of earthquake while he had watched Christ die on the cross. Large sections of Jerusalem were destroyed, and seven thousand of the leaders of Israel who had participated in the execution of the two men of God were killed. They had been partying one minute; they were dead the next. The city of Jerusalem cried out in terror, and even acknowledged God, but the majority of the citizens of earthly Jerusalem still refused to repent and believe in heart.

The pause after the sixth trumpet had ended. John had seen what had been happening with God's people for the first half of the tribulation. They were being persecuted, even killed because of their faith. But God promised justice. What John had seen gave the believer another foundation of hope. God's justice meant He would provide for those who follow Him. That justice also meant a profound woe for the ones who continued to turn away from His mercy.

Then the seventh trumpet sounded. With its blast came a fast-forward overview of the rest of the tribulation period. John was quickly given a glimpse of the ultimate victory of Christ. Man's plans for establishing a paradise on earth would fail. God's people would be drawn together. There would be a time of reward for all believers, including those saints who lived during the times of the Old Testament and the believers who would live during the tribulation. There would also be a time of judgment for the ungodly. Then there would be established a new heaven and a new earth, perfectly made without the threat of sin anymore.

But the highlight of this overview was a new view of the throne room of God. As John watched the place of worship in heaven opened and access to God was shown to be unrestricted. God showed John that finally man and God had perfect fellowship. All the promises of God to Adam, to Abraham, to the nation of Israel, to David, and to so many more would be fulfilled.

The items used to testify of those promises from the rainbow, to the Ark of the Covenant, to the nail-scarred hands could be seen. Worship broke out once again in heaven, for God is great and mighty. His mercy for His people would endure forever. But before all of this came to be, there was the final act of godless man to be played. It was an act that would last three-and-one-half years and would plunge man into the depths of sin and despair. It was an act heralded once again by the mighty thunderings and voices of God, a warning that the atrocities of the past would be intensified and that if it were not for the intervention of Christ, man would destroy himself and all of the world.

References:

Daniel 9:27; Jeremiah 31:38-39; Psalm 2:9; Psalm 23:4; Daniel 7:25, 12:11; 1 Kings 18:28; 2 Kings 1:10; Matthew 27:51-52; 28:2; Matthew 17:1-13

Chapter 12

Revelation 12: 1-17

The seventh trumpet had sounded. As John prepared for the final scenes of history to play in front of him, his vision took a new turn. John was about to be shown the history of a war that would peak during the last three-and-one-half years of the tribulation – a war between Israel and Satan, between God and one of His former archangels, and between believing man and the "deceiver" of all ages. Suddenly there appeared an important figure, a woman with the same brightness as the previous angel from God. Clothed in this brightness she appeared to be standing on the moon and had a hair ornament of twelve bright, shining stars.

John was aware of only one woman clothed like this. From Scripture he recalled the vision that Joseph had expressed to his father and brothers, a vision of the sun, the moon, and eleven stars bowing down before him. That vision had culminated in Joseph's being taken captive by his brothers and sold into slavery. But it was also the vision that showed one day Joseph would lead his family. The name of that family was Israel. This woman appearing before John was the symbolic presence of the nation of Israel, God's covenant people.

As John looked closer he noted that the woman was pregnant and gave birth with tremendous anguish. The child she bore was none other than the Messiah. The promise and birth of the Messiah had indeed caused the nation of Israel intense pain. History displayed a long list of persecutions this nation had been through because from her the Son of God would come to save mankind from its sins. Why had this persecution been perpetrated? John saw another figure that would answer that question. It was the figure of a dragon with immense power, intelligence, and beauty; indications of which were in his appearance with seven heads, ten horns, and seven false crowns. John was seeing Lucifer, the archangel who had now become the archenemy.

As beautiful as the dragon was, John was quick to record that he was also totally red in color. Satan was a creature who delighted in shedding blood—an evil, dangerous murderer of man. His appearance indicated that he had a vast following. The ten horns did not simply mean power but a power base in the governmental organizations of man on earth. His following was enhanced by successfully persuading one-third of the angels in heaven to follow him in his war. The main strategy of that war had been to destroy God's creation, especially man. That strategy, to be successful, also included successfully disposing of God's promised Messiah. That meant getting rid of Israel.

Satan had tried to do just that from the day of Abraham to the time of Christ. He had used the Pharaoh of Egypt in trying to kill the Hebrew male children when they were born. He had employed the pagan nations to attack openly the young nation of Israel. He had utilized and was almost successful in inducing the nation of Israel to destroy itself in sin. Then when the time of the actual birth of the Messiah arrived, he had used Herod in killing the male children of Bethlehem. Satan had even personally confronted Christ, tempting Him in the wilderness and continuing that temptation for all of Christ's time on earth. He thought he had won when one of the disciples, Judas by name, betrayed Christ. He had even had a brief celebration when he watched Jesus die. But the reality of what had happened soon came to life when Jesus Christ was resurrected from the grave. This action of Christ was like a steel pole thrust through Satan's body. It was a warning from Christ that all who followed this dragon would end up like him, shattered for eternity. Christ had ascended after His resurrection, the victory of God insured. He would return one day as the commander of a host, a mighty army of God that would consummate that victory.

Satan has known he would lose the war, but he has remained determined to carry as many of mankind as he could with him into his awaiting kingdom of hell. He has continued his campaigns against man, Israel, and now a new enemy organization, the Church. To assault the Church Satan stepped up his activities. John observed as Satan stood before God accusing the members of the Church, the true believers of their sin. Each time he made an accusation, Christ would step forward and assert they were not guilty because He had paid the price for their sins. It was a scene John had read about when Satan made similar accusations to God's friend named Job. Just like he did with Job, Satan had persisted down through history making accusations about individual men and women to God.

When Satan was not successful in his accusations to God, he would in turn go and accuse man of his sins. Here he would meet more success, as Christians, relying on their own strength and not their armor of faith and prayer, would be incapacitated and even permanently crippled spiritually as they believed the lies of this master deceiver. They would live in guilt, not victory. They would live as the conquered instead of as conquerors. Satan's severest work against the Church would be to make the true believers so weak and defeated that no further conversions would be made into faith. John was amazed, yet he knew that even as he watched, Satan was accusing him of sins to God. Satan was thorough and vigilant in this work. John had assurance that although the accusations might be legally correct, they were spiritually forgiven by grace and faith.

These campaigns would intensify during the tribulation. The Church would be gone, but Israel would remain, reminding Satan of the past and tormenting him with the knowledge of the ultimate victory of God. He would try to destroy Israel. If he could succeed, he would show God's promises to this nation to be a lie, God to be weak, and himself (Satan) to be a real contender for the throne. John observed as Satan now accused the tribulation believers of their sins before God. For thousands of years this had been going on. Finally, with the sounding of the seventh trumpet, this part of Satan's war would end. A battle broke out in heaven. It had happened before when Satan had first rebelled against God. But after that battle he had still had access to heaven to make his accusations. With this new battle his access would be cut off, and there would be a heaven free of the whining voice of the old serpent.

The battle in heaven was intense, involving the strongest members of the opposing forces. God's army was led by Michael the archangel who had always had charge of protecting Israel. Daniel had encountered this angel before after he had fought through the forces of evil to present God's message to the prophet. Even in the time of Daniel, this angel had had a difficult time getting through, spending three weeks trying to deliver the message. Through the persistent prayer of the man of God, Michael finally conveyed the message. Michael was given authorization to use all of his forces and power, including the prayer power of the saints, to rid heaven of the presence of Satan. The battle was not easily won, but Michael prevailed, and Satan was forever banished from heaven. No more would his accusations echo in the ears of God.

John acknowledged in his heart that until that day of banishment, followers of Christ would have to maintain their battle lines. With Satan making his indictments both to God and to the individual Christian, believers would be locked in a spiritual warfare that can only be won by using the offensive and defensive spiritual weapons of war provided by Christ. John's brother in Christ, Paul, had called those weapons the "whole armor of God" (see Eph. 6:10-17). The main offensive weapon in that armor was prayer.

The victory in heaven by Michael had immediate results. Satan, in a demonic rage, was now confined to an earthly kingdom. He decided to inflict as much damage as he could on God's people, taking out his hate of God on those who loved Him. Now all of mankind, both the believer and the unbeliever, would be subject to a highly concentrated barrage of the unholy presence.

In heaven the results were the exact opposite. The silencing of the accusing voice led to a renewed worship of an even greater intensity than before. The salvation of mankind won on the cross was one step closer to becoming perfected in God's holiness. As John rejoiced in this celebration, the actions and words of the worship going on revealed to him how to maintain the assurance of salvation, even in the worst of times. This worship centered on remembering—the blood of Christ shed for man, the victory of Christ in defeating sin and death, the coming defeat of Satan and evil, and the authority of Christ in all matters. He who has the power and authority to take the scroll of God and establish the literal and permanent Kingdom of God, also has the power and authority to keep those who believe in Him.

The jubilee in heaven was still going on, when John's attention was refocused on the outrage of Satan trying to drown out the followers of God on earth. The Antichrist was now fully indwelt by Satan, his power consolidated and his fury complete. Out of the mouth of the Antichrist, under the direct orders of Satan himself, came a series of orders to send out a flood tide of persecution. The orders of the Antichrist were to overwhelm and destroy any follower of God, but to specifically concentrate on those followers from Israel. Giant masses of mankind, that looked like a tidal wave of destruction, quickly complied with the orders.

The persecution resulted in the believers' fleeing for their lives. John watched as many were caught, tortured, mutilated, and murdered. But many more were given a special divine protection that would lift them out of harm's way with the speed and agility of eagle's wings. These protected followers would continue to vocalize the clear and ever-present words of the truth of God. Scattered across the wilderness of a world of sin, they will spend the last three-and-one-half years being fed physically and spiritually by God. It reminded John of God's provisions for Israel during their wilderness journey of forty years when their clothing did not wear out and food fell from heaven on a regular basis. As severe as the persecution of the Antichrist was, John could not help but rejoice as he viewed the constant provision of Almighty God for His people.

References:

Genesis 37:9-10; Micah 5:2-3; Isaiah 66:7-8; Daniel 7:19-25; Daniel 8:10; Psalm 2:9; Ephesians 6:12; Job 1-2; Zechariah 3:1-2; Luke 22:31; 1 John 2:1; Jude 9; Daniel 10:13; Daniel 12:1; Exodus 19:4; Matthew 24:16; Isaiah 8:7-8

Chapter 13

Revelation 13: 1-18

The description of the first two characters involved in the war between God and Satan had helped clarify many concerns. Before John could understand the next actions of God, he would have to be introduced to some other personalities involved in the conflict. The introduction he received was frightening.

As he watched, John saw Satan call a special disciple of his from the massive sea of humanity. This one person would be Satan's special tool to seize control of earth, deceive mankind, and try to set up the kingdom of Lucifer. He would look to many like an answer to prayer, the long-awaited Messiah. But he would in reality be the exact opposite of Christ and would be known by believers as the Antichrist. John had known personalities like this in his life, but the one he was meeting now was the embodiment of all the attributes of Satan himself.

Satan chose this man at the beginning of the tribulation, when the world was suddenly without the influence of the true Church because of its rapture. For three-and-one-half years this selected instrument had worked to gain power and assume control of the world. He had done his job well. John described this Antichrist in words similar to those given by the prophet Daniel. His appearance was grotesque, yet intriguing. He had seven heads, showing his complete knowledge and leadership of man. He had ten horns, showing an earthly power base of ten governments he had succeeded into seducing to follow him, either through political finesse or outright force. A further indication of this power base was shown in ten crowns. These ten governments had given their authority over to this false messiah.

John was most explicit in one part of his description of this man. His name was "blasphemy." He claimed the authority and position of God. He claimed to be at least the equal to God, if not God Himself. John knew that Scripture had given this man many names, including the King of Babylon and the Man of Sin. But John wanted no doubt in his name. He wanted everyone to know this imposter was the Antichrist.

To John this man was the horrible mutation of the beasts that live in the heart of demonic man. John recalled that Daniel also saw this beast-like man. Calling forth the same animals Daniel used to describe Satan's kingdom, John showed that this Antichrist was the ultimate of all of Satan's followers. He moved like a leopard, quickly conquering the world and establishing a new culture and glory based on man's power and wisdom. He had the power of a bear to purposefully trample down any who would stand against him. Those who followed him, he held in the vise-like grip of a bear hug. He had the stealth of a lion, springing traps upon any he desired to make his prey. Those traps were laid through trickery, magic, and sorcery. Once trapped there would be no escape. The combination of the three beasts was awesome, but John beheld in this man a forth beast, one that could not be identified with any of the known animal kingdom. It was a massive, powerful, all-consuming creature with no compassion or pity and a desire only to please itself.

The disciple of Satan was awesome, his appearance monstrous, his power gargantuan. In addition to these, though, the Antichrist had one special feature. John saw that at some time in his rise to power the Antichrist had been mortally wounded. Through some trick or deception, he had appeared to be resurrected. It was his highest claim to being the Christ. This trick would give the Antichrist a weapon to counter the claims of Christ. It would be a show of his power to balance the real resurrection of the two witnesses, a resurrection that the whole world had witnessed. Satan and the Antichrist were working to refute every claim of Christ, God, and the believers. The resurrection trick would be one of the most impressive.

Through the Antichrist John watched the majority of mankind start to worship Satan. The masses of humanity would proclaim the Antichrist as their only hope. He would promise peace, joy, abundance, and a society that would be nothing less than a utopia. Through the power of his electrifying speech he would brainwash a sick and sinful world into believing that he was the answer to all of their problems—but a few would recognize the truth. In the midst of the lies would come the voices of truth, the proclamation of God's Word by the believers. Their words would fall mainly on hardened hearts and deaf ears, but they would fearlessly tell all that this leader of the world was nothing more than a puppet of the devil. Their efforts would unleash severe persecution on them, but their voices could not be silenced.

The message of God was clear to John. Those who follow God have eternal life. Those who refuse to believe do not. Their names would not appear in the Book of Life. Into this book God had placed the names of every living soul. During each soul's earthly life, in some way, God would reveal Himself and offer each soul at least one clear opportunity to recognize their sins and need to follow Him in faith. The names of those who accepted that offer would remain in the book. The names of those who refused to accept that offer and died without choosing to follow God would be erased from the book. The Antichrist was making fictitious claims of a utopia for those who allied with him. God promised an inheritance of heaven with all rights and privileges of being His child for those who believed in Him.

The persecution of the believers by the Antichrist would become worse with each passing day of the tribulation. John was given a special message for the tribulation saints. God urged them to have hope. As powerful as this man seems, God would always be in control. Everything that was happening had a reason behind it. Not only were these believers to have hope; they were also warned not to resist his evil actions with force. Their patience and faith would carry them through. For a believer to retaliate would bring further persecution. More importantly the believer's actions should testify of his faith in God. Vengeance, retribution, and justice were God's private domain.

Having been introduced to the first beast/man, John was appalled to see a second beast/man. Where the first had been called by Satan from the massive ocean of humanity, this second man was called from the nation that claimed to be God's people, Israel. This man looked like a lamb, with limited power and authority as shown by having only two horns. John saw no crowns on his horns and knew that meant he had no governmental power. He was a religious leader, with the voice of Satan. That voice was pleasant to the ears, but deadly to the soul as it uttered only lies. This second man of Satan was the False Prophet. His power and influence over people would cause them to worship the Antichrist and in the process, Satan. His words, actions, and appearance all show his devotion to the Antichrist.

As John watched this anti-evangelist he noted again that the Antichrist had the appearance of having been killed and resurrected. John's emphasis of this was designed to warn his readers that even Satan's host can work miracles. But all miracles are not from God. Those of Satan are deceptive events that are designed to impress man but not to strengthen him. The false prophet had a whole inventory of miracles he could perform. Christ had warned His followers of these powers in the hands of deceivers. They would impress many and lead many astray. Satan's followers had used them in Pharaoh's court to impress the nation of Egypt. They would use them again to impress the nations of the world. As impressive as they were, John was sure that there was one miracle this man could not perform. He could not provide the miracle of salvation.

The false prophet worked quickly with the Antichrist to unite the world under their control. At the right moment, he declared the Antichrist the only God. To seal this declaration he had erected in the Temple in Jerusalem an image of the Antichrist. All mankind watched as this image was unveiled. Then the false prophet worked one of his biggest miracles. He made the idol of the Antichrist talk. This statue gave orders that tested the faith of the believers and increased their trials. For anyone to buy anything from groceries to real estate, they had to give their allegiance to the Antichrist. This pledge would be shown in bearing his symbol or mark. To live you would have to have that mark. People by the millions lined up to be tattooed with "the mark of the beast."

John was clear that believers would recognize the Antichrist and his ways. The true believers would have no doubt in their minds as to what was really happening. The mark of the beast would show itself to be the mark of the unholy trinity, man's mark of failure and sin, combined with his stubborn, selfish, egotistic nature. John equated that mark with three sixes, a trinity of falling short of the perfect number seven. Where the Holy Trinity of God the Father, Christ the Son, and the Holy Spirit were perfect, the unholy trinity of Satan, the Antichrist, and the false prophet fell short of the glory of God.

Somewhere in the back of John's mind there had been a nagging question. It was a question that would come up time and again in believers' minds and hearts down through history. Why does God allow Satan to continue to exist? Why will man continue to go through the trials and temptations? Why will God allow Satan this kind of power to deceive the masses? With this part of the Revelation, John had part of the answer. God was allowing Satan his chance to prove himself. Satan has constantly told man he has a better way, that God is the real liar and that he can provide for man better than God.

Allowing Satan to live and even to temporarily rule the earth will reveal the truth. Satan is a liar. God was also allowing man a choice. God never wanted man to be forced to obey Him. God's desire for fellowship with man was based on man's desire to follow God. John had made the choice for God. He prayed once again that others would see the truth and that it would truly set them free from the craftiness of the master deceiver, Satan.

References:

1 John 2:18-22; Matthew 24:24; Daniel 7:1-20; Isaiah 14:4; Daniel 8:9; 2 Thessalonians 2:3-11; John 5:21-29; Exodus 7:11-12; Mark 13:22; Daniel 9:27, 12:11

Chapter 14

Revelation 14: 1-20

The descriptions of the unholy trinity, their power, and the persecution of the saints evoked the need for a return to the scene in heaven. John's heart skipped a beat as once again he saw Jesus. This time Jesus was standing in the City of David, Jerusalem. With him were the 144,000 special envoys that had been sealed by the Spirit during the opening of the seven seals. The guiding voice from heaven told him that he was seeing the end of the seven years of tribulation. This part of his vision was to leap ahead in time, showing the triumphant Christ and all those who had given their lives to Him united in victory. That victory precipitated another time of worship. With harps and songs heaven accompanied the 144,000 in a new hymn of praise, a hymn only these persecuted tribulation believers could honestly sing.

John could not help but observe that all 144,000 were there. Here, at the end of the tribulation, stood all who had followed Christ. Christ had not lost a single soul. Their chorus of praise proclaimed that very fact. They had been redeemed, sealed, and brought home to victory. During this songfest, John spotted some new details of this unique group. They had remained single during their earthly lives. They had not become burdened with the impedimenta of earthly life, so they could be devoted to the things of a heavenly one. There was nothing wrong with marriage, but for these chosen ministers during the pressure and turmoil of the tribulation it was best that they not have the additional concerns of marriage and family.

Their celibacy also taught another spiritual lesson. As they had remained physically single in their lives, they had also remained spiritually single in their devotions. Their lives were not without sin, but because of the power of Christ, they were remarkable in their faith, testimony, and works. Their lives were a springboard for others to leap into the arms of God in faith. They were the first results of God's mercy in the tribulation, but they were not the last.

They were a marked contrast to the followers of the Antichrist. Where John noted that all of the Antichrist's ways were lies, there could be found nothing close to falsehood in these ambassadors for Christ. The remarkable fact was that even their speech was truthful. They spoke only the truth, even when that truth might result in their arrest and death. They could have very easily lied about their devotion to God and their revulsion at the very thought of the existence of the Antichrist. At times those lies would have put food in their stomachs. But even when hungry, facing torture and death, these men refused to compromise the truth. Because of their faith, their testimony, and their love, God looked upon them as He looked upon every other believer. They were without fault because His Son had paid the price of their sins.

Attention was suddenly drawn to an angel flying through the skies of the earth. This angel started to preach the Gospel, and the message went out from him to every man in every nation. It was a clear and simple sermon, a last chance for salvation, a final plea for people to believe in God and forsake the ways of the devil. It was unusual to see an angel preaching. Nowhere else could John remember angels presenting the Gospel message like this. Up until this time, it had been man's privilege and duty to proclaim the Gospel. The angels had always desired to do this.

After all, one of the reasons they had been created was to be the elite messengers of God. But God had wanted man to perform the task of presenting the Gospel. It was for man that His Son had died, and it would be up to man to spread the good news. However, times had changed. What John was observing was the beginning of the end of the tribulation, its last three-and-one-half years. The Antichrist, with his power consolidated and fully indwelt by

Satan, would move with a new zeal to terminate the believers in God. Those who spoke out would be quickly eliminated. It would be almost impossible and definitely suicidal for man to preach the Gospel. God was protecting His believers, but He also wanted to have the Gospel proclaimed one last time. This angel was given the task all the other angels had wanted – to preach to man the Word of God.

Quickly the message was given. "Fear God and worship only Him. Do not fear those who can take your earthly life, but those who can take your eternal life. Do not take this message casually. The time has come to choose. Choose the One who created everything." It was the final invitation. John did not indicate if anyone was moved by the message. He left the readers to their own interpretation. Many would want to think positively and presume that huge hosts of people came to embrace the Lord as Savior. But the truth might very well be that sinful people had gone so far in sin that they would never again consider following God.

A second angel followed the heavenly evangelist. This one bore a different message, a message of prophetic doom for the city of Babylon. This angel talked as if this city had already been destroyed. It would exist for two or three more years, but God had already signed the demolition orders. He would not change His mind. The city was as good as gone.

God had held a special judgment for this city since its organization under a man named Nimrod. This earthly king had dared to proclaim himself equal to God, had led his people astray, and had even tried to assault heaven by building a tower. Although the physical assault would never succeed, God had recognized the potential of a spiritual assault that would lead all mankind to defeat and death. Since the days of Nimrod, Babylon had stood as the control center of any and all who would lead men away from God. Satan had used this city to his advantage. For the sins she had allowed to be committed in her city limits, sins that amounted to spiritual adultery, this city would pay a steep price. The angel repeated his prophecy, showing that two cities of the nature of Babylon would be destroyed. One would be a religious capital. The other would be a governmental and commercial capital.

A third angel came rapidly into view. Where the first had proclaimed the Gospel, this angel proclaimed the law. Every man would be judged based on their relation to one or the other of these proclamations. Those who rejected the Gospel would be forced to drink the wine from the fruit of their labors. With all their labors bearing the fruit of fleshly sin, the wine would be the wine of God's wrath. God had allowed that wrath to build. He had been patient with all mankind. Multiple chances had been given to change their fruit from fleshly to spiritual. The constant refusal had resulted in an overflow of God's wrath at the end of time. That wrath would mean judgment by Christ and the sentence of that judgment would be eternal existence in a literal and fiery hell. The angels of heaven would carry out that sentence by tossing each guilty person into the lake of fire from which there is no escape.

As those who refused God are given their punishment, those who accepted God would be rewarded. John's view of the future judgment was interrupted by a voice from heaven, saying that those who are martyred during the last half of the tribulation, before the second coming of Christ, would receive a special blessing because of their faith and the difficulty of maintaining that faith in such a sick and corrupt environment. That blessing would include rest from the terrors of the persecution and recognition by Christ of their struggles and works.

The angels had delivered their messages. The vision of Christ and the 144,000 in Jerusalem had faded. Now John beheld Christ again, but this was not a vision of the victory at the end of the tribulation. John now perceived how that victory had come into being. The Christ he now observed was authorizing the final judgment, the final wrath of God to be poured out upon the earth. Christ was sitting on a cloud, wearing a crown and carrying a sharp sickle. The physical description revealed judgment, the reaping of the harvest of souls. John recalled a special message Christ gave one day during His earthly ministry, forecasting this harvest. At the end of time, He would authorize His angels to gather in the souls of all people. Those who believed would be protected as valuable and good. Those who did not would be burned as stubble and chaff.

A second harvest was observed. The first had shown the separation of good and evil mankind. The second showed the judgment of the evil. The symbolism was not wasted on John. The prophets Isaiah and Joel had also foreseen this day. They had equated it with the harvest of grapes, when the grapes are gathered in and placed in a huge vat. Then the keeper of the vineyard would jump into the vat and stomp the juice out of the grapes. In the process some of the juice would inevitably splash up on the vineyard keeper's robe. The harvest of grapes showed John that those who rejected Christ would be collected and judged. Their blood would be required of them because they had not accepted the blood of the Savior. Their blood would be shed because they were guilty of shedding the blood of God's Son and God's people. Their blood would flow because their sins had built to overflowing the cup of God's wrath. They would be trod under His feet, their blood would flow freely, their lives squashed in His righteous judgement. The blood would be so thick it would splash upon His garment.

John was seeing the climactic battle between God and evil. Not far from the gates of Jerusalem this battle would be raged. Masses of human lives would be trampled down, so many that the blood would flow four feet deep for over 150 miles. John would later identify the site as the Mountain of Megiddo. History would acknowledge it as the Battle of Armageddon.

Why was this carnage taking place? The God that John wrote about in the Gospels was One who so loved the world that He gave His Son. Had God changed? No, God would always be the same. He still loved mankind; He still wanted to forgive. But as great as God's love for man might be, it could never overlook His abhorrence of sin. All that could ever cover man's sin is for man to accept God's love by believing in Jesus Christ as personal

Savior and Lord. John saw the judgment that awaits. He hoped that what he related in his letter would open the eyes of those who were never actually saved. He hoped that fear and love of God would work together to increase the harvest of lives that believed in God. As much as he hoped, it remained for the individual to decide for or against God.

References:

Matthew 24:19; 1 Peter 1:10-12; Revelation 17–18; Matthew 13:37-43; Isaiah 63:16; Joel 3:9-17

Chapter 15

Revelation 15: 1-8

John had observed with a mixture of elation and depression the final victory of Christ and His judgment of those who had refused salvation by grace through faith. The identification of the principal characters of the war between God and Satan and the prophetic scenes of the end of the tribulation period had provided a brief break in the unveiling of history. Now, with John's mind once again focused on that unveiling, the Spirit showed John the preparations going on in heaven for the final series of judgments and plagues that would be known as "the wrath of God."

Man's sin was complete, and His rebellion against God was total. Man's heart had become completely hardened to any of the pleas from the Throne of Grace to turn from his wicked ways. John saw seven angels who carried seven bowls. The angels were standing in heaven. Their appearance was a sign of the end of the time of grace. For sinful man there was now no hope. Yet, for the redeemed of heaven the appearance of these seven envoys elicited another wave of worship.

John had seen the area before the throne of God early in his Spirit-led journey. Before it had been a sea of smooth crystal, a sign of the presence of the redeemed of God who had been brought into His presence. At the time he first observed the crystal sea, it was clear. Now John was shown that sea once again. It appeared to be filled with fire. Present now in the sea of the redeemed were those who had been martyred by Satan through the Antichrist. They had endured the fires of persecution and prayed for justice from the Almighty Judge of the Ages. John's attention was being drawn to them so he might be assured that

God had heard their prayers and the prayers of all the saints through the ages for divine justice. These believers were now at peace. In their arms were the harps of rest and harmony in the arms of the Lord.

With the horrors they had endured John was somewhat astonished that from their lips came songs. John recognized these songs. One he had learned from the rabbis. The other he had sung with the disciples after the ascension of the Master. The martyred followers of Christ were singing the song of Moses, a song of deliverance from bondage, and the song of the Lamb, a song of the power, holiness, and righteousness of Christ. John's amazement came from the fact that, with all that these wonderful people had endured, they could still sing. He had seen people who had been through far less persecution in the Church who would never open their mouths in song.

Many was the time he had seen small incidents of trial create festering cancers of bitterness in the lives of professing church members. Compared to what he had seen these tribulation saints endure, those incidents were vacations on the seashore. When would those who claimed Christ learn that with Him, bitterness, jealousy, envy, the holding of grudges, and the seeking of revenge were alien to life in Him. How he wished that these two songs would be highlighted in the church hymnals.

The last chords of the special music echoed across the fiery crystal sea of tribulation believers. From the Holy Place of worship, the inner sanctum of the Throne Room where the Throne of God was guarded by the four creatures, the seven angels moved forward. They were clothed in uniforms similar to what Christ wore. The difference in their uniforms from that of Christ indicated they were performing duties similar to those of the priests of the Old Testament. They proudly wore these uniforms of purity and power.

As they were given the seven bowls of the wrath of God, John detected something familiar in the area of the throne room. He was seeing the original pattern of the Holy of Holies in the Temple at Jerusalem. In the Holy of Holies, from the era of

Moses to the time of the Babylonian Captivity, had been the Ark of the Covenant. It was representative of the Throne Room now gazed upon by John. Its lid was considered the throne of God and called the Mercy Seat. On this lid once a year the blood of the offering of atonement was poured. The mercy seat covered three special items to the nation of Israel: the second copy of the Ten Commandments, a jar of manna, and the rod of Aaron. These three items were a constant reminder of the sins of man. The Ten Commandments gave the law which man had broken even before they were delivered by Moses to Israel. The first edition had been shattered by Moses as a sign of that transgression. The pot of manna reminded them of the provision of God which time and again they had rejected for what appeared to be the more flavorful provisions of the world. The rod of Aaron was a reminder of their rejection of the leadership God had provided for them. Israel had always thought they could elect a better leader than God. They had rebelled against Moses and Aaron, and that rebellious nature had continued all the way past their turning against Jesus hundreds of years later.

These three items had been covered by the Mercy Seat. God had given Israel a splendid model of the throne room. For sinful, rebellious man there was mercy for those who would accept the poured-out blood of the Lamb of God. The only requirement was for man to humble himself and believe in that shed blood. From the beginning of time to now there was the availability of grace and mercy.

But now John saw that come to an end. The fact that these angels were coming out of the throne room showed they were moving away from God's gracious presence. The role of the priest had been to move into God's presence to seek mercy for the people. These angelic ministers were reversing that role. They were moving out to execute God's justice. John not only saw the angels moving out, he also saw the Holy of Holies opened and the lid of the Ark removed. There was no more mercy between God and sinful man. Sinful man had had his last opportunity of grace, mercy, and salvation.

To give that truth a final emphasis, John now looked at the area that had been set aside for grace and mercy, blocked off. The presence and power of God became a barricade that no man, angel, or spirit could move or penetrate. John's heart ached at the reality of an end to the age of mercy. So many he had talked to had presumptuously relied upon God's grace never ending. They had claimed an all-loving God who would never send a soul to hell. There would always be a chance to reach God. What John viewed now was God's truth. God's mercy and love are everlasting for those who believe in Him. For those who do not, there is an end of that mercy and love that is given the name "hell."

References:

Revelation 4:6; Exodus 15:1-21; Deuteronomy 32:1-43; Revelation 5:9-12; Exodus 39:8-14; Deuteronomy 10:4-5; Numbers 17:10; Hebrews 9:4; Exodus 16:33-34

Chapter 16

Revelation 16: 1-21

The voice of Christ gave the final orders of the tribulation. One by one the seven angels moved out to deliver the contents of the bowls of the wrath of God. The period of time during which these bowls would be poured out on the earth Christ had called the time of great tribulation. It was the time of the direct and specific judgment of God upon Satan, the Antichrist, the False Prophet, and their kingdom.

As the first angel poured out the contents of his bowl, an odor of rotting flesh immediately permeated the air. The contents of this bowl afflicted all who followed the Antichrist with putrid, incurably spreading skin diseases. The affliction was so great that no place could be found that did not have the stench of putrefied flesh. It caused pain and was so horrible to look upon that man could not bear to see his own image. This was much worse than the affliction of boils on Pharaoh at the time of the Exodus. When Moses recalled that plague he had warned Israel that a worse plague would fall upon unrepentant man. This plague was even greater than the previous plagues during the breaking of the seven seals. The sins of the flesh had resulted in their judgment.

The second angel tipped his bowl over the earth, and all the seas turned to blood. Pharaoh had seen the Nile turned to blood, and during the first part of the tribulation man had experienced one-third of the sea becoming blood. Now, with God's wrath complete, all the sea became blood. Unbelieving man had proclaimed that all life came from the sea through an explainable evolutionary process. Now God turned the so-called source of life into a cesspool of death.

The air was filled with the smells of disease and death when the third angel emptied his bowl upon the earth. Immediately all the fresh water, from the mighty rivers to the cool springs, turned into blood. Any chance of relief from the plague of skin disease by bathing in cool, clear water was now gone. With this pouring out of this bowl there came an unusual endorsement.

As John watched the waters run red, he heard an angel proclaim how just this judgment against man was. John identified this angel as the one God had placed in charge of the waters. This angel had watched his duties and responsibilities vanish in this judgment, but knew that man was getting what he deserved. He had taken the lives of many of the believers. He had shed their blood. Now in turn they would have only blood to drink. With the endorsement of the angel came a hearty "amen" from the martyred saints.

The fourth angel poured his bowl upon the earth, and suddenly the atmosphere became super-heated. People were subject to a heat wave that was far beyond anything on the record books. It seemed to take the world by surprise, but man had been given multiple warnings of this judgment. Moses, Isaiah, Malachi, and even Christ had tried to warn man that continuation in sin would literally provoke the heat of God's wrath. The first four bowls combined made life on earth grotesque. With skin disease and no water, yet intense heat, there could be nothing but misery. Man was sampling a form of hell, eternal physical torment with no relief. Even with this sampling, man's heart was unbreakable. He continued to blaspheme God.

The fifth angel's bowl was emptied. Suddenly the sun dimmed. Everywhere the Antichrist ruled was now dark. Spiritually they had loved the darkness. Now, physically, its reality caused them even worse pain. John had read in Scripture about this type of painful darkness. Immediately before the Passover, God had stricken Egypt with a similar darkness. He had then warned man that He would do it again if he continued in sin. God's prophets—Isaiah, Joel, Nahum, Amos, and Zephaniah—and Jesus had all given notice of this expression of God's wrath.

Man was supposed to live in God's Light. When man denied that Light, God gave him the darkness. Still man denied the existence or providence of God.

As the sixth angel poured out his bowl, John saw the Euphrates River dry up. This river that flowed in Babylon had always been a natural barrier between the nations of the East and the nations of the West. It was on the Eastern shore of this river that John had seen the mighty army of 200 million men assemble earlier in the tribulation. Their intentions had never been clear. They claimed to be allies of the Antichrist, led by his demonic cadre. Now the Antichrist found himself at their mercy. Quickly, in a series of propaganda lies, the unholy trinity broadcast promises, pledges, and treaties trying to maintain the unity of their earthly kingdom. The first six bowls had shown them to be far less than they claimed. Their kingdom was in shambles. Revolt was in progress by leaders from nations to the South and North of Babylon. Catastrophic war was already taking place. This army of 200 million now moved without restraint to add further confusion to the state of affairs of man's world.

While the unholy trinity tried to verbally mend fences, Christ issued His last statement before His return. It was a warning to unholy man. It was a promise of blessing to redeemed people. He was coming suddenly, without further warning. For unholy man He would not be a welcome visitor. Unholy man desired for Christ's coming as much as he would a thief to come and take away all his treasure. In reality that is what Christ would do. Unholy man had invested his life in earthly treasure. Christ's coming would take all that treasure away. Redeemed man had made a different investment. He desired Christ's coming because with it his treasure would be realized.

With the final words of Christ came the final battle of the tribulation war between God and man. That battle would be fought in Israel in the area of a mountain named Megiddo. John called the area Armageddon. That battle would destroy all mankind, except for the intervention of Christ. That intervention would not occur until the delivery of the seventh bowl.

The seventh angel poured his bowl into the atmosphere. The judgment of God upon sin-filled earth was complete. For the second time John heard a familiar voice cry, "It is finished." He had heard similar words from Christ on the cross as He proclaimed the completion of His mission to provide salvation. Now that voice claimed the completion of the mission of judgment. With that completion the whole world shook. The foundations of all the earth were moved. Every village, town, and city became rubble. This earthquake centered in Jerusalem. The City of David was broken apart. All around the world other cities and governments were destroyed. Of special interest in this destruction was the city of Babylon, the capital city of the kingdom of the Antichrist. God had reserved a special judgment for this city. John was shown its inevitable end. Shortly God would give him the details of this special wrath.

The earthquake caused mountains to collapse, islands to disappear, and the world to flatten with the weight of man's sin. From the sky there came giant chunks of hail weighing over one hundred pounds each. Men everywhere fell under the weight of these icy stones. It would seem that now people would recognize God, would fall down and beg for mercy and an end to this judgment. There was pain, disease, tragedy, and even death, but still man's heart remained harder than the hailstones that pummeled his head. Instead of turning to God, man turned further away than before. Instead of claiming God, man continued blaming God. The earth was effectively destroyed not because of God, but because of man.

The only One who could turn this around was Christ. Through all of this He was in control. Amazingly, through all of this He had provided for those who accepted Him as Savior and who were still alive on earth. As global as these judgments had been, they did not touch the believers. They remained safe in the care of their Lord. John rejoiced that he knew that security. Nothing would ever separate him from the love of God in Christ Jesus. He could only pray that others would see the disaster of living outside that love.

References:

Deuteronomy 28:15-18; Exodus 7:20-25; Deuteronomy 32:24; Isaiah 24:6; Malachi 4:1; Luke 21:25; Psalm 121:6; Exodus 10:21-22; Isaiah 60:2; Joel 2:1-2,31; Mark 13:24; Daniel 11:40-45; Titus 2:13; John 19:30

Chapter 17

Revelation 17: 1-18

Angels twice had proclaimed the destruction of Babylon. The first proclamation had been a prophetic one before the pouring out of the seven bowls of wrath. The second proclamation had been immediately after the seventh bowl had been poured into the atmosphere of the earth. Both times the angels making the proclamation had been purposefully repetitious in stating that Babylon had fallen. As John watched the results of the seven bowls, one of the angels involved in their delivery approached him to explain the reason behind God's special judgment of that city.

From the beginning of time, in the area near the Euphrates River there has been some sort of organized civilization existing near the site of the city of Babylon. As mentioned before in that region Nimrod had desired to build a tower to heaven, trying to demonstrate that he was equal to or better than God. When God confused the language of Nimrod's people, confusion set in. From that confusion of languages the area was called Babel, changed later to Babylon or the land of Babel. From that time forward Babylon had been synonymous with rebellion against God and confusion. Time and again the kings of the area around Babylon had led in assaulting God's people and God's ways. Babylon had been representative of any individual, group, nation, or power that was opposed secretly or openly to God. It was the capital of the kingdom of the Antichrist and Satan.

The angel now showed John there were two Babylons, a religious Babylon and a governmental/commercial Babylon. Both were cities whose inhabitants stood against God. Both were judged by God and destroyed—one in the middle of the tribulation and the other at the end of the tribulation during the pouring out of the seven bowls of wrath. The angel led John to a vantage point where he could first survey Babylon. John immediately recognized the view. He was looking at Rome, the city built on seven hills.

Quickly his guide pointed out that this Babylon was the religious one. Controlling this city was a harlot, better known as the false church. God had always described people who professed Him, but in reality followed the world, as spiritual "adulterers" or "harlots." After the rapture of the true church there had been left behind a false, worldly church. John had seen the beginnings of this bogus church in the letter Christ had written to the church at Pergamos. This church had compromised with the world to the point that God called it a harlot. The church was supposed to be the Bride of Christ. This church had become the prostitute of the world, the Antichrist, and Satan.

From her beginnings she had been powerful and even beautiful to man. She had accrued riches beyond compare. Her buildings for worship had been adorned with the wealth of the world's adoration. Yet with all her wealth, people were still living in poverty. The Church that Christ had desired was one that helped the poor, hungry, and needy. This church was one that stockpiled its wealth at the expense of the poor, hungry, and needy.

She appeared outwardly to be royalty, clothed in purple. She also showed that she survived by the shedding of innocent blood. Red—the color of Satan, war, and bloodshed—was also prominent in her apparel. For many years she claimed to be the true church, but for those years she had done nothing but seek her own glory. To gain power she had made filthy and heinous agreements with the world's powers. She had sought to control all mankind, claiming the ability to approve and deny salvation depending upon the works of the individual. She had even taken in many other religions of man, becoming a vast conglomeration of religion and giving birth to all sorts of misguided concepts about God, Christ, Mary, and salvation.

She was no more than the madam of a huge brothel of false religions. She had been successful in getting multitudes of people from every area of the world to believe in her. Because of these violations of her fidelity to Christ, she had been given a multitude of names. All exposed the truth that she sought to be God herself. She denied her own glory and power, her own kingdom. She dared to display the name of Christ as her own on her head, but in her heart the names all equaled blasphemy. She claimed to have mysterious powers and visions proving her authority from God. John knew that the mystery of God's kingdom and authority had been revealed in Christ. The only mystery involving Christ was the exact date of His return.

Those who stood in her way, good Christian men and women who recognized her falsity, had been martyred. The untrue church had claimed it was a cleansing inquisition. God knew it as abominable murder. As John comtemplated this false entity, and what she had succeeded in doing to vast numbers of people, he was speechless. Those she had not killed, she had brainwashed. The more she grew in power and numbers, the more intoxicated she became with her own power. When the real Church disappeared, she moved in rapidly, claiming that this was part of her plan. At the same time the Antichrist, needing some help in consolidating his power, allied with her. John saw this female impersonator using the Antichrist, riding him like a horse. He also noticed that the horse was becoming tired of its rider, preparing to throw her into destruction.

The angel reinforced the vision of the Antichrist with a renewal of his symbolic traits of power, intelligence, and control. This repeating of these traits (seven heads, ten horns, etc.) showed how the false church had duped itself into thinking she was in control. Quickly her control and power eroded into the hands of the Antichrist. Using his power to sway people with words, the Antichrist started blaming the troubles brought on with the breaking of the seven seals and the blowing of the seven trumpets on the false church. It was not a new tactic. Six other times in history, men trying to set up kingdoms had verbally or literally assaulted God and His kingdom. The Egyptians, Greeks, Persians, Babylonians, and Assyrians had all turned on God and His people. John was seeing this revelation as the Roman Empire was trying to purge itself of Christianity. The false church was a seventh attacker of God's Kingdom. It appeared for a moment that the Antichrist was an eighth, but his use of the false church made him a continuation of their attack. Now he turned on the very one who had helped him gain power. The Antichrist had an intense hatred for anything remotely associated with God's Kingdom. Although the false church was not part of God's Kingdom, her professed association with God was enough to find her guilty by association.

The Antichrist passed his hatred on to his followers, and they quickly formed mobs that decimated those who were leaders and dedicated followers of the false church. The destruction of her disciples was done with such frenzy that they tore them into literal pieces and then to desecrate her further, indulged themselves in a cannibalistic feast on the remains. God had judged the false church and the city of her power. It was a spiritual Babylon, no matter what its physical name might be. For a short period of time the false church and her capital city had enjoyed prominence and power over widespread portions of the earth. Now the false church was destroyed, and the city that once boasted her glory was left in ruins. Amazingly, God had judged this city by letting the Antichrist destroy her. She was another example of the truth of God's Word, "Whatever you sow, that shall you also reap" (see Gal. 6:7). She had sown spiritual adultery. The punishment for adultery, according to God's law, was death by stoning, a death that would tear the body to pieces.

References:

Isaiah 1:21; Matthew 19:21; Jeremiah 44:15-20; Ezekiel 8:13-14; Ephesians 3:1-9

Chapter 18

Revelation 18: 1-24

The destruction of the false church by the Antichrist was greeted by the world with elation. They had grown weary of the hypocrisy, the holier-than-thou attitude, and the meaningless ceremony that obviously had not kept tragedy away. The false church's claim of authority from God had definitely been shown to be a lie by the troubles ushered in with the breaking of the seven seals and the blowing of the seven trumpets. The Antichrist had succeeded in consolidating his power and now moved to what he thought were bigger and better things – control and domination of the earth.

From the writings of the prophet Daniel, John calculated that the Antichrist would experience rebellion in his own ranks at the end of time. His promises of peace and prosperity would constantly be broken by the truth of God's righteousness shown in the judgments that would keep falling upon earth until Christ returned to stop them before everyone and everything were destroyed. The Antichrist's confederation would fall apart under the stress of these judgments. Daniel had seen a war break out in the final half of the tribulation. Rebellious kings would fight the Antichrist, and that war would culminate in one dramatic battle called Armageddon. John had experienced that battle in his vision when the sixth bowl of wrath was poured out. Before that great battle, the Antichrist would watch his center of power destroyed by God. That center of power was a city called Babylon, a second Babylon of man's government and commerce.

An angel now approached John to show him the reasons and reality of the destruction of the second Babylon. Announcing the destruction of the capital of Satanism, the angel told John that the destroyed Babylon would become a prison for demonic spirits and a haven for vultures cleaning the bones of the people who had died in its destruction. The reason for this special annihilation was because this city had been the center of materialism, worldliness, decadence, and the occult. She was extravagance and opulence personified. In her could be found every worldly pleasure twisted into gross sin. The world loved this city because she had given man wealth, happiness, pleasure, and thrills in fleshly terms. But what she had given man would not last. Like all works of the flesh, the city was doomed for destruction.

As the angel showed John the extent of this Babylon's sin, another voice from heaven was heard with a warning to believers. They were to flee Babylon before she was destroyed. What were believers doing in Babylon? God's Word was constant in its admonition that, although a person has to live on planet earth, he does not have to live in its sinful ways. Time and again believers in God had been seduced into the world's ways. The warning given by the angel was very similar to the one given to Lot and his family to exit Sodom. Lot had hesitated to leave that city of sin because he became comfortable in its luxuries. Apparently believers in the last part of the tribulation would fall for the same trap. This warning by this special voice was designed to wake them up. God's mercy for His people was shown again as unending. Now His judgment for those who refused to become part of His family would be shown to be dreadful.

The city of luxury and indulgence was about to be given her wages from God. For this city those wages would involve a bonus. She had proclaimed an "eat-drink-and-be-merry" morality. Now the tomorrow of her death had arrived. John viewed this destruction by fire, just as Sodom and Gomorrah had been obliterated. The destruction of this city was sudden and rapid. Her existence ceased in one titantic flash, and her loss would be felt by all.

The world, in her sorrow at the loss of the center of worldliness, gave this city a funeral. Headed by the leaders of government, the procession of mourners included all the salesmen and brokers of the world. It included all who had given their lives to a job or profession and worshiped success and position rather than God. It included all who thought they lived by bread alone, all who gave more importance to what they had in their bank accounts, their safe deposit boxes, or even their cupboards, rather than what they had in their hearts. All who were status conscious—who kept up with the Joneses, who concentrated more on what they wore than what they believed or who placed more importance on control and power of other people rather than being controlled and empowered by the Spirit of God—participated in the funeral for Babylon. They were even joined by those who thrived from delivering the worldly goods to all mankind. From the heads of state to the local stock clerk and delivery man, the whole world had seen its god and center of life destroyed like a rock dropped into the sea. One moment the city was there, and all was well. Next even the ripples of her existence could not be found, but the waves of her destruction could still be felt.

Because Babylon was gone there was no more music in the world. Music symbolized happiness and without this center of commerce there was no more happiness. In heaven the saints were singing new songs. On earth not even the old ones could be heard. Because Babylon was gone, there was an economic depression. White- and blue-collar workers were now standing in unemployment lines with no hope of ever getting another job. The promises of the Antichrist for abundance and joy were now shown as lies. His continuing promise to do something about the situation was overshadowed by his preoccupation with a war going on in his own ranks. He was more intent on moving troops to Palestine to quell the rebellion than he was moving the economy. Because Babylon was gone, even the lights of the world darkened. There was no more glitter and glitz, only darkness. The end result of sin is always darkness.

Her sins had brought her destruction. Pride and arrogance, spiritual deception, and corruption were the foundations she had been built upon. Those foundations were shifting sand. To those sins she had added the persecution of believers and the purposeful and willful misuse of God's blessings. Success, self esteem, and the senses were gifts of God. Man had misused them and made them into gods. Now the end had come.

References:

Isaiah 13:6-7; Zechariah 5:5-11; Revelation 14:8; Matthew 7:24-27

Chapter 19

Revelation 19: 1-21

Choruses of "Praise the Lord" filled the air. From every corner of heaven shouts of salvation, love, honor, and praise radiated. Each accolade proclaimed His virtue, His love, His grace, and now His righteous judgment. From the masses of the crystal sea to the Church and the angelic chorus, the message of praise combined into a crescendo of "Alleluia! For the Lord God Omnipotent reigns." The time of the end of the tribulation and the return of Christ to set up His earthly kingdom had come. No more would creation groan from the results of sin. The weight of sin had been lifted. Love, peace, joy, wholeness, and harmony would reign. The reality of that generated a new phase of heavenly choral praise no human had ever heard before.

A wedding had taken place in heaven, the wedding of Christ to His bride the Church. The parables of the wedding feast and the ten bridesmaids that Christ had told in His earthly ministry had been verified. Christ had gone to claim His Bride at the time of the rapture. Many had been caught unprepared for that event. He had returned to His Father's home for the ceremony. That ceremony had been beautiful. The Bride had been dressed in a double gown. One of the gowns had been given to her by the Groom, a pure white gown of righteousness. Now John saw another gown, also white in color. But this gown was adorned with jewels. Each jewel had been carefully sewn on the gown by the Bride. Each jewel represented the works done by the Church in the name of Jesus. The bridal gown was adorned with memories of acts of love done for and in the name of the Groom. The ceremony had been beautiful, the joining of Christ and His Bride.

The Apostle Paul had foreseen this beauty when he claimed that at that time believers would be face-to-face with their Redeemer. Now that the official duties had been handled, He could proceed with His bride to their wedding feast. Like any Groom, Christ desired to show off His Bride's beauty. That display would start at the wedding feast. John actually became so wrapped up in the beauty of the scene that he mistakenly started to give praise to the angelic messenger that was guiding him through it. The angel quickly corrected John and focused John's praise and vision back on Christ.

In John's day the feast after the ceremony was held at a place prepared by the groom. The extravagance and length of the feast depended upon the wealth of the groom's family. Those invited to the feast were highly honored. The names on the list of honored guests at the wedding feast of Christ would include all those Old Testament saints and all the tribulation saints.

Now John watched the Groom move to prepare the banquet hall, planet Earth. Heaven opened for a second time. (The first time was when John saw Christ coming for His Bride at the time of the rapture.) Christ was now seen coming on a white horse, a sign of war. He was coming as the leader of a mighty army to rid earth of sin and its results. With eyes like fire that could penetrate to the depths of the heart and soul of man, searching for truth and justice, He quickly put an end to the Battle of Armageddon. His involvement and control of this battle were shown in His blood-stained robe and His multi-crowned head.

It was quite a contrast to what John had seen in Christ's earthly ministry. Then He had entered on a donkey, a sign of peace. Then He had worn a crown of thorns. Then the blood that flowed was His. Then He was the suffering servant sent to seek and to save. But He was not returning as the meek and lowly servant, the scapegoat and sacrifice of God. Now He was King of kings and Lord of lords. With His spoken word which was like a sword that could strike with authority any who would stand against Him, He rapidly placed all the world under His rule. His spoken word had created the world. Now His spoken word would end the destruction of it and lead to the earth's restoration. The wicked had been slain. The righteous had been spared, and with another spoken word the earth was restored and the banquet hall prepared. The wedding feast of the Lamb of God that would last for one thousand years was about to begin.

At the same time, there was another feast that had already started. Armageddon had ended in victory for Christ, but that victory involved the death of millions of the followers of the Antichrist and his faithful companion, the False Prophet. The physical bodies of this slain multitude now provided a feast for the vultures. They had come to the banquet hall in filthy garments, the garments of sin. Because of that they were cast out, a sign of the death of their bodies and the confinement of their souls to the place of torment, later to be released for final judgment. However, there were two whom Christ judged immediately. The Antichrist and the False Prophet, because of the enormity of their rebellion against God, were immediately thrown into the lake of fire, known as hell. They had led the world astray. Their eternal separation and torment in the fires of outer darkness would start immediately.

There were two feasts, one about to start and the other already going on. The Wedding Feast of the Lamb would be filled with joy and excitement. Present would be all the believers whose faith had guaranteed their participation. It was a feast prepared by the King for all who were part of His kingdom. The second feast was the death feast of the dragon. Present were the vultures of the air. It was a feast prepared by the refusal of man to believe and the constant hardness of his heart. The invitation of Christ was to attend His feast. John saw that one way or another everyone would attend one feast or the other. The choice was between being the honored guest or the main entree.

References:

Romans 8:18ff; John 3:29; Ephesians 2:4-10; Matthew 22:1-14; Matthew 25:1-15; 1 Corinthians 13:11-12; Isaiah 63:1-16; Revelation 14; 2 Thessalonians 2:8; John 1:1-14

Chapter 20

Revelation 20: 1-15

Christ had made the preparations for His wedding feast. Before it could actually begin a couple of matters remained to be done. On His command an angel appeared to escort the greatest party crasher of all time from the scene. Satan had already destroyed the initial party of man in the Garden of Eden. Undeniably, man had had a part in the whole mess by consenting to Satan's rule and apparently even enjoying it. Christ now made sure that Satan would not have anything to do with His wedding feast. The angel carried a chain and a key. With the chain he quickly bound Satan. Unceremoniously he deposited Satan into the bottomless pit, to remain there for the entire time of the feast, one thousand years. With all the power Satan had possessed in the past it was comforting to see that now he had none. In the presence of the glorified and Almighty Christ, Satan can do nothing but cower and shake.

Earth had been reborn. Satan and sin were no longer present. Now Christ moved to usher in His invited guests. John watched as there suddenly appeared the saints of the ages and the believers martyred during the tribulation. In the third phase of what Christ called the first resurrection, these Old Testament saints and tribulation believers were given new bodies to unite with their already-present souls. This resurrection had been started by Christ's own resurrection, His being the first phase. The second phase had been the resurrection of the believers of the Church when Christ raptured the Church. Now all who were part of the body of believers were present for the wedding feast.

The invited guests were given thrones, along with those who were part of the wedding party. Each member of the Kingdom which Christ had re-established would have an important function. Christ did not need their help in running the Kingdom. He simply desired their fellowship. It had been His desire that all of His people work together from the beginning. With sin and Satan present, that had never been a possibility.

The earth had been replenished. God's promise to Abraham of a nation of vast numbers was now a reality. God's promise to David of a throne occupied by one of his descendants forever was now fulfilled. What the disciples had desired, the establishment of Christ's Kingdom, had taken place. For one thousand years there was peace. The instruments of war no longer existed, only instruments of production. Swords and spears were now plowshares and pruning hooks. Harmony existed everywhere. Old "natural" enemies were now the best of friends as lions and lambs roamed freely together. Disease and death, pain and suffering had been banished. Everywhere there was abundance, love, and peace. Everyday was one of worship and praise. And in the midst of it all was Jesus, guaranteeing a continuation of this ideal environment.

In this ideal environment new children were born and raised. Many had entered into this environment who had not died during the tribulation. Their offspring now began to multiply in astronomical proportions. They showed a startling nature. Even in this perfect place, where everything had been restored, man's heart was afflicted with rebellion. These children did not want to live in this Garden-of-Eden world with Christ. They did not want His reign and rule. The attraction of sin was still present, even though Satan was not. Every man born must make a choice either to follow Christ or not. These born during the millennium would be given their opportunity to choose at the end of the thousand years. Until that end, everyone continued to enjoy and prosper under the government of Christ.

It was a wonderful time, but it came to a close. At the end of the one thousand years Christ released Satan once more. Now the day of choosing had come. Many followed Satan in one last attempt to dethrone Christ and kill His followers. The rebellion contained the same hatred John had observed during the tribulation, the same hardness of heart and stubborn self-will. It was sinful man at his worse. Satan led these spiritual descendants of Israel's old enemy, the nations of Gog and Magog. But the rebellion had not even organized itself well before fire fell from the sky and slaughtered the participants.

Satan was pulled from the carnage and taken in front of Christ. There he received His final sentence, eternity in hell with its two other infamous occupants, the Antichrist and the False Prophet. Among many in John's day there was the idea that Satan came from this hell and actually enjoyed it. John saw in Satan's reaction that he had no desire whatsoever to go to the place where there would be only weeping and wailing and gnashing of teeth.

Satan, the Antichrist, and the False Prophet had received their sentences. Now Christ moved from His throne on earth to the heavenly throne of judgment, a great, white throne, taking His place on this seat of pure justice. Then the second resurrection occurred. This was the resurrection of the unsaved, the unbelievers of all time. The great and the small, the rich and the poor, the powerful and the weak; all who had refused to follow God whose souls had been residing in the place of torment called hades, were now escorted in front of Christ. Their physical bodies were made immortal and united with their souls. Now they would be tried by Jesus to see their eternal fate. Why was this trial going on? Why did Christ not sentence them as He had the other three residents of hell? Because Christ is just. He will check the record of each person's life carefully and allow them to give a defense of their lives. After searching the facts and hearing the defense testimony, each unbelieving person will then be shown why he will not be allowed into the new heaven and earth prepared by Christ.

In front of Christ stood each believer. Christ now opened several books of testimony about the believer. In one book was the law of God, testifying as to man's sin. In another were the recorded words of the individual, both good and bad. The excuses they had given for not following Christ or being too busy or doing it some other day were recorded there. In another book were all the works of the individual, both good and bad. All the charity, all the personal love, all the deeds done to better mankind. Also recorded there were the real reasons behind those works; personal glory, recognition and even tax write-offs. Recorded too were the secret works and thoughts of each person. In front of Christ there were now no secrets in anyone's life. Still another book used was the book of conscience. This book showed that each man had had a revelation of God and His love in some way. Even with that revelation, they had refused to follow God. All these books and more were there to help Christ judge each unbelieving person. But the most important book was the Book of Life, in which the names of all who believed were recorded. In the end, no matter how good the records of each person's life looked in the other books, if their name was not in this one they were condemned.

Each person came, stood, pled his case, had the evidence presented, and waited. Christ carefully inspected the Book of Life and looked up. The look was unmistakable. It caused the knees of the accused to buckle and from their lips would come the statement of fact, "You are the Christ, the Son of God!" But the statement of fact was too late. If made in life it is a statement of faith and fact. Made now, at the judgment throne, it was a fact that would only condemn them. With tears in His eyes, in a voice certain in its justice and just as certain in its compassion, the words of truth would come forth. "Depart from me . . . I never knew you." In darkness they had purposefully lived. Now in the outer darkness of the second death they would forever remain.

For the believer there was but one death to be experienced. For the unbelievers there were two. The second death was the eternal separation from God in the place of unending torment. Death never meant the end of existence. It means existing without God. The horror of the judgment, the sentence, and the second death was crushing. One after another, vast multitudes were thrown into hell with no hope of pardon or parole. With the arrival of each new occupant, the volume of the wailing increased.

None of the believers were present during this judgment. The horror of seeing anyone, much less the horror of seeing friends and family members cast into this eternal damnation, would be too great for any believer to bear. Greater still would be the shock of having one of those condemned passing by on his way to hell, looking into your eyes, and saying, "Why didn't you tell me? Why didn't you try one more time to tell me? Why didn't you try harder to show me in words and deeds the truth of Jesus Christ?"

John knew that the love of God needed to be presented to all mankind. Along with that love, there needed to be given the whole truth. God so loved each person that He gave His Son to die in their place so they would not have to experience this second death. But that sacrifice only applies to those who believe on Him. God's love is great, but God's justice is true. In grace He provided salvation. Those who accepted that provision were saved for eternity. Those who did not accept it were condemned for the same eternity. "The wages of sin is death, but the gift of God is eternal life through Jesus Christ our Lord."

References:

Genesis 12:7; Galatians 3:16; Isaiah 40:10; Acts 1:6; Revelation 9:13; Isaiah 24:21-22; Daniel 12:1-3; Isaiah 26:19; 1 Corinthians 3:4; Matthew 19:28; Matthew 20:23; Isaiah 19:22-25; Isaiah 2:4; Isaiah 11:6-9; Isaiah 65:20; Isaiah 35:5-10; Joel 2:26-27; Joel 3:18; Isaiah 51:11; Exodus 23:26; Isaiah 9:3; Zechariah 3:10; John 5:22-29; Ecclesiastes 12:14; Matthew 16:27; Romans 2:15-16; Matthew 12:37; Galatians 3:10; Ephesians 4:8-10

Chapter 21

Revelation 21: 1-27

In a micro-second everything changed. There was no more scene of a judgment seat. There was no more of the old earth. Earth was totally changed. There were no divisions in the continents, no seas to separate nation from nation, man from his fellow man. All the effects of sin had been removed from the planet. All of life on earth had been made new. Christ had told John while walking in the fields around Galilee that this day would come, a day when there would be a new earth and a new heaven.

The changes of the earth were awesome, but the changes of heaven were more marked. The combination of these changes were so dramatic that John had to remind himself he was actually seeing what would transpire. He knew he was seeing something brand new, so beautiful and brilliant that it could only be the work of Christ. Coming down from the sky was a city so large that it seemed like a whole, new planet. As it positioned itself in the skies of the new earth, John heard a voice from heaven. This was the New Jerusalem, the capital city of God, the center of all creation. It was a city more beautiful than any bride John had seen, because it was the dwelling place of the Bride of Christ. In this new city God would live, and man would live with Him. Now, God's original desire for mankind had been completed. Now God and man could live together physically. They could walk together, talk together, and laugh together. However, there was one thing God and man would not do together. They would not cry. In this new creation of God there were no more tears, no more pain, no more death, no more separation, no more arguments, no more hurt feelings, no more misunderstandings between God and man, or between man and his fellow believers.

Another voice was heard and John instantly recognized this voice. It was the Master, the Messiah, his closest friend, Jesus. The One who created all things had now made all things new. God's final steps in His plan for humanity had been taken. Now Christ repeated a name that He had used at the beginning of this revelation to John. "I am the Alpha and the Omega." When He had used this identity before He had employed the abbreviated form of the word for the letter "omega." Now Christ used the full form. The intent was clear. At the beginning of this journey, Christ had not completed the final steps. The omega part of the name had not been accomplished in its entirety. The salvation won on the cross had now been finalized for eternity. For those who had a desire, a thirst for God, their thirst would now be quenched forever. For those who had claimed faith in Christ, followed Him, and loved Him, all of heaven was their inheritance. Christ was not giving them just one mansion. All of the universe now was under the joint partnership of all of the family of God.

The creation of the new heaven and earth did not affect one area of the former creation, hell. Just as believers would inherit all of the universe for eternity, all unbelievers, no matter how bad or good their lives had been, would inherit all of hell for eternity. There was no second chance. There was no re-creation of hell to lessen the pain. There was no probation or parole. The souls of those who refused to humble themselves, to repent, to change their wicked ways, would remain in the hell of fire, brimstone, and darkness.

An angel came up to John, reminding him he indeed was still being led by the Spirit of God. Taking his arm, the angel guided John to the best vantage point to see the place prepared by Christ for His Bride. John now viewed with a mixture of joy, praise, worship, and continuing awe the city designed and built by the Master Carpenter. As he approached it, he noted that from every point of the compass, light radiated from this new colossal city. It was like looking upon countless diamonds, with the light refracted into colors beyond any rainbow he had ever seen. The city was built on a square foundation. Around the city was a wall with twelve gates, three on each side. No matter from what direction someone approached the city, they would have easy access. The twelve gates were named, one for each of the twelve tribes of Israel. It was a reminder of access to God being first promised to the patriarchs and being finally provided by One who descended from those patriarchs.

The walls were placed on twelve foundations, each foundation named for one of the twelve apostles. The foundation of the city in which the Church, the Bride of Christ, would dwell was laid by those twelve wonderful men. They had given all for their Lord. They had followed Him, learned from Him, and then deserted Him. But His love and grace conquered all in their lives, and they went on to insure that the good news of the Gospel went out to all mankind. They gave their lives for Christ. Paul had mentioned their devotion and sacrifice in his letter to the church at Ephesus. Their work was instrumental in the coming of this day. They all built upon the foundation of Christ and in the process their lives became part of that same foundation.

John was now shown a golden measuring rod. With careful precision he and the angel measured the city. It was 1,500 miles long, 1,500 miles wide, and 1,500 miles high. It had more space in it than the moon that had previously circled the earth. The wall that surrounded the city was 216 feet high. The wall was made of diamond, the hardest and most beautiful of all natural substances. The city itself was built of gold, but not the gold John had seen on earth. This gold was clear. Everywhere he looked, he could see through the materials that had been used in building this city. The light of God radiated through the city to all the universe. John realized that in this city of clear gold, not only would God's light be seen, but man's former need for barriers, walls, and doors to protect himself and his secrets would no longer be necessary. In this New Jerusalem, everyone would want to be with everyone, with no secrets to hide and no desires to gossip or tell tales.

John moved from measuring the city back to observing the construction. He saw that the twelve foundations were made of twelve different jewels. Their colors of gold, red, blue, and green blended to make a kaleidoscope of beams of light. The twelve gates were constructed of pearl. John remembered Jesus' many stories of pearls and their value. The gates to this city had been opened by His giving His life. They were gates for which an enormous price had been paid. They were opened because of Christ, and now they would never be closed.

Connecting the gates and going throughout the city was one street. It too was made of clear gold. Connecting all areas of this massive city to its center around God, this one street reminded John that there was only one pathway to God. Christ had warned people that that road was narrow and difficult to find in life. Now in eternity, this one street was bright, wide, and beautiful.

The New Jerusalem had everything. From every angle and from every area there was brilliance, beauty, peace, and joy. It did not have a church, a temple, or a place of symbolic worship. The sanctuaries of earth were no longer needed. The symbolic worship of the past, done in the Spirit of God, was now the true worship of infinity, done in the immediate presence of God. There was no need for a sanctuary, for now God and man could meet face to face.

The new earth had its light from the New Jerusalem. God provided the light for all His people. On earth, Israel lived in a true Promised Land. Between earth and the New Jerusalem there was a steady procession of worshipers from the leaders of nations to the everyday citizen. There was no concept of time. Worship in the New Jerusalem went on continually, and no one ever tired of it, complained of having to go, or had the remotest thought of giving some weak excuse to God for not coming to praise His name. The gates to the city were open. All who desired could approach God at any time. The constant worship seemed to bring a greater glow to the city, as the radiance of God's love was compounded by the praise of God's people.

It was all new. The earth was truly paradise, a planet that flowed with milk and honey. The New Jerusalem was a glowing gem in the sky, a continual honeymoon setting for the Bride of Christ and a center of praise for all of renewed creation. There was no more sin, no more filth in words, deeds, or thoughts. Those who had their names forever inscribed in the Book of Life written in the blood of the Lamb of God now enjoyed eternity with God, His Son, and their family in Him. Christ had left the old earth hundreds of years before to prepare this place. The hands that were pierced had built this place of eternal bliss. Those who never took that hand in faith would never come close to getting in. Those who had taken that hand in faith would always get in and never have to worry about leaving again.

References:

1 Peter 3:10-12; Matthew 24:35; John 14:2-3; 2 Corinthians 5:17; Revelation 1:8; Romans 8:16-17; John 9:5; Ephesians 2:19-20; Matthew 13:45-46 John 1:4-5; John 8:12; John 12:36,46

Chapter 22

Revelation 22: 1-21

Brilliant and beautiful, the New Jerusalem hung in the sky like a perfect diamond, set in pure gold and displayed on the most beautiful of all women. John's description of the New Jerusalem had included precious metal and gems. Those components alone would be cold and lifeless. The New Jerusalem was far from cold and lifeless. Flowing down the center of the street of gold, in a clear, cool, gleaming flow, was a river of life-giving water. It originated from the thrones of God and Christ and flowed throughout the city, giving access to its contents to everyone.

Time and again John had heard Christ talk about eternal waters that never ended and provided for all the thirsts of man. Christ had described them in spiritual terms. Now John saw that those waters were also eternally physical. All life came from God originally and would continue to come from Him for all eternity. The plagues that John had witnessed which had turned the water on earth into blood would be no more. The blood of Christ in the lives of all the Kingdom citizens would guarantee that the water of life would always be clear, clean, refreshing, and free.

On the banks of the river John spotted an unusual tree. Nourished by the waters of life, this was the tree of life. Its root system followed the course of the river throughout the city, and the tree actually appeared as multiple trees lining the river. It was all one tree, constantly in bloom and bearing fruit. However, the fruit was not all the same. With each passing month the fruit changed, giving a variety to all who would come and eat. Life in Christ is never dull. His life is constantly changing and always refreshing.

Life in the New Jerusalem would not be routine, with a dull, monotonous diet and the same schedule of events and worship day after day. In His presence the newness of life would not dissipate like the fragrance of spring. It would increase and develop in fresh and innovative ways with each passing day. The leaves of this tree John wrote were good for healing. In an environment with no sickness, sorrow, or death, this seemed like a useless function. But those leaves of green, that were taking in the direct light of God—turning it into nourishment and bearing fruit—were testimony of each believer's life. Each had been exposed to God's light, accepted it, and now had eternal life. But that eternal life was not supposed to be stagnant. It was supposed to be used to provide nourishment to the entire body of Christ, bringing forth fruit that tasted like love, joy, peace, patience, kindness, goodness, faithfulness, meekness, and gentleness. The leaves of healing showed that now all who lived with God were whole in Him.

The river of life and the tree of life completed the presence of the Trinity of God in the New Jerusalem. God the Father and God the Son were obviously present, with their thrones in the heart of the city. Now the water and the tree showed the Spirit of God functioning as He always had, quenching the thirst of God's people and bearing fruit for their lives. Now the Spirit flowed freely, and all the fruit was available for every person. Now, with sin no longer present, the Spirit would no longer be bottled up or stagnant. Man, in his sin-filled life, could quench the Spirit. Man, in this God-filled life would find his thirst for all the things of God quenched.

Man and God were together forever. Unending worship and praise would be conducted without fatigue or boredom. Christ's promise of man ruling with Him forever had been made real. Believers would see Him face-to-face, would know Him by all His names, and He would know them by theirs. Never again would even the shadow of darkness enter into His follower's lives. The brightness, the glory, and the joy of life would now be complete. And it would last forever and ever.

The scene of the New Jerusalem would never disappear in John's mind. God had revealed that scene, along with all the others, so that John could relate them to everyone. He had experienced what had not yet happened. Those who did not believe in Jesus Christ as their Lord and Savior, who could still read and hear this revelation from God, still had a chance. Christ was coming again, quickly, suddenly, without further notice. Christ repeated this combination of a promise and warning. Three times he had given it at the beginning of the vision. Now again he repeats it three more times. For those who read, heard, and followed His revelation by believing in Him, there was a special blessing. They would have eternal life with Him. They would have the blessing of sharing in His ministry on earth until He does return, the privilege of telling others the good news of salvation. They would have a closer walk with God, empowered and indwelt by the Holy Spirit. They would have eternal rewards in heaven.

It was not some sort of nightmare that John experienced. God, in His love, gave one more plea for man to come back to Him. That plea, that revelation, caused John to once again make the mistake of worshiping an angel, the messenger of God. Quickly the angel corrected John. It is not the messenger that man should worship, but the one to whom the messenger and his messages points. It is not the preacher, the pastor, the church, or its traditions that should be worshiped, but the Son of God. It is not even Scripture or the gifts of the Spirit that are to be worshiped, but the Savior, who is Christ the Lord. John learned to be careful to make sure exactly who he was worshiping. Maybe some of his readers would see that they too were worshiping the *things* of God instead of God.

Carefully, John was to write about what he had seen. He was to deliver it to all people, so that they might know the truth. Those who still refused to accept God's revelation, who would scoff and claim it was all fiction, would be forever doomed. Those who did accept it would be forever blessed. As Christ would be forever eternal, their fate or reward would be eternal. When He comes again, that fate or reward would be sealed. The choice was up to each individual. They could follow Him and have free access to Him, face-to-face fellowship with Him, forever. They could refuse Him and remain inhabitants of hell forever.

John heard one final word from Jesus. The fact that He identified Himself as Jesus showed that He was speaking now as Savior. He was the Promised One from God, the Messiah promised to Adam, to Abraham, and to David. He fulfilled all the prophecies of old and went beyond them. His first coming was like the shining of the first star of the morning. It was a bright glow in a darkened world. It was a promise that soon, very soon the Eastern sky would light up in a blaze of glory. Soon, very soon, He would come again, and the day of His coming would never end.

To these words the Spirit of God and the saints in heaven gave their invitation. Their desire was for Christ to return, now if possible. But their desire was also that man would return to Christ. Now it is possible. John was to make that message clear. He was not to add to or take away from God's message of salvation. He was not to increase or decrease what is necessary to have salvation, to know that you will one day reign with Him in the new heaven. Salvation would always be by grace through faith. People could never do any works to earn their way into heaven. At the same time, if truly saved, people would be about the works of God. Because a person was saved, it did not mean he would never sin again. But because a person was saved, it did mean that he would never love sin again. God loved each person so much He gave His Son to die in their place, to pay the price of their sin. But God's love will never supersede His righteousness. Man is given the opportunity to accept salvation. If he refuses that salvation in this life, He will never have a second chance from hell.

Christ promised John that He would come again, suddenly and soon. To that promise John added his amen and desire that He come, even now. But until He did come, John remembered that he had a job to do. To him was given the revelation of God, the unveiling of heaven, the new vision of the eternal life promised by Christ. He would deliver that message even to us with the last words a prayer: "May the grace of the Lord Jesus Christ be yours."

It was not just some old man's dream. It is today's reality. Rapidly we are moving through history to the day when Christ will return to rapture His church and set the events of Revelation into full motion. The vision of John was for the people of God. The question remains. Are you absolutely sure you are part of God's family? Have you opened your heart, repented of your sins, invited Him in as your personal Savior and Lord? If you are not sure of your salvation, make sure today. If you are sure, then together, all Christians have a job to do for the Lord. John wrote his vision down so we might experience what he experienced. If we genuinely believe in what he experienced, if we too have experienced them, we will not merely sit around, staring into the sky, speculating on when He will come. Now is the time to praise Him, to practice for the pure worship to come. Now is the time to learn more about Him, because He loves us. Now is the time to follow Him, to move into new areas of discipleship, to set new goals of purity, and to claim new power from His Spirit. Now is the time to tell others, "Behold, He is coming soon!"

My prayer is that the Revelation of God, Jesus Christ, is your personal Savior and Lord. May His grace be your salvation so that one day we might meet in the place He has prepared for us and share for eternity His love.

References:

John 4:14; John 7:37-38; Ezekiel 41:1-2; Zechariah 14:7-8; Genesis 2:15-17; Ezekiel 47:12; Galatians 5:22-23; 1 Thessalonians 5:19; 2 Corinthians 1:22; Ephesians 1:7-14; Revelation 2:5, 16; Revelation 3:11; Deuteronomy 4:2; Deuteronomy 12:32; 1 Corinthians 2:1-5; 1 Thessalonians 2:2-5

Notes

Allen, Clifton J., Editor, *The Broadman Bible Commentary,* Vol. XII, (Nashville, TN: Broadman Press, 1972).

Alpha and Omega Ministries, *The Preacher's Outline and Sermon Bible* (King, NC: Christian Publishers and Ministries, 1991).

Caffon, B. C., *The Pulpit Commentary*, Vol. XXII, (Grand Rapids, MI: William B. Eerdmans Publishing Company, 1950).

Graham, Billy, *Storm Warning,* (Dallas, TX: Word Publishing, 1992).

Jeremiah, David, *Escape the Coming Night*, (Dallas, TX: Word Publishing, 1990).

Larkin, Clarence, *Dispensational Truth*, (Glenside, PA: 1920).

Lindsey, Hal, *There's a New World Coming,* (Santa Ana, CA: Vision House Publishers, 1973).

McGee, J. Vernon, *Thru the Bible with J. Vernon McGee,* Volume V (Nashville, TN: Thomas Nelson Publishers, 1983).

The New King James Bible, (Nashville, TN: Thomas Nelson Publishers, 1985).

Robertson, A. T., *Word Pictures in the New Testament,* Volume VI (Nashville, TN: Broadman Press, 1933).

Shoemaker, H. Stephen, *Retelling the Biblical Story* (Nashville, TN: Broadman Press, 1985).

Tuck, Robert, *The Preacher's Complete Homiletic Commentary,* Volume XXXI (New York: Funk and Wagnalls).